On Suicide

On Suicide

A DISCOURSE ON
VOLUNTARY DEATH

Jean Améry

TRANSLATED BY JOHN D. BARLOW

Indiana
University
Press

BLOOMINGTON AND INDIANAPOLIS

This book is a publication of
Indiana University Press
601 North Morton Street
Bloomington, IN 47404-3797 USA

http://www.indiana.edu/~iupress

Telephone orders   800-842-6796
Fax orders   812-855-7931
Orders by e-mail   iuporder@indiana.edu

*The publication of this book was made possible
through a grant from Inter Nationes, Bonn*

Library of Congress Cataloging-in-Publication Data

Améry, Jean.
[Hand an sich legen. English]
On suicide : a discourse on voluntary death / by Jean Améry ; translated by
John D. Barlow.
p.   cm.
Includes bibliographical references.
ISBN 0-253-33563-9 (cl. : alk. paper)
1. Suicide.   I. Title.
HV6545.A5713   1999
362.28—dc21   98-53904

1 2 3 4 5 04 03 02 01 00 99

The world of the happy person is a different one
from that of the unhappy person.
Just as with death the world does not change,
but stops.

—Wittgenstein,
Tractatus Logico-Philosophicus,
Propositions 6.43 and 6.431

Contents

TRANSLATOR'S PREFACE

In this translation I have basically followed the principles indicated in the "Translator's Preface" to *On Aging*, although translating *On Suicide* has been considerably more challenging. Specific issues are explained in the notes. I would like to thank Indiana University-Purdue University at Indianapolis and Dean of the Faculties William M. Plater, as well as the School of Liberal Arts and its Acting Dean, Miriam Z. Langsam, for enabling me to take an administrative leave to work on this translation. Although I alone am to blame for any lapses in the pages that follow, I am grateful to John Gallman, Director of the Indiana University Press and the editor I worked with, for being, as always, extremely helpful and a pleasure to work with; to Kathleen Babbitt, Jane Lyle, Michael Lundell, and Jeffrey Ankrom for their advice and assistance; to Bill Schneider, Professor of History at IUPUI, for responding to questions about the translation of Améry's French passages; and to Pat Barlow, for suggestions about the manuscript and for providing innumerable forms of help and advice.

This series of interlocked essays was originally broadcast on the radio by Jean Améry in 1976 before it was published in book form. Readers should be advised at the outset that it is not an apology for self-destruction or a brief for assisted suicide, although it is unmistakably a defense of the freedom of individuals to define their own destiny and have the right to die by their own hand. Much of the book's argument is directed toward collective morals that condemn self-annihilation, such as those of religion and social pressure, as well as social and psychological interpretations of suicide that inadvertently impose standards of behavior by defining and categorizing individual actions. Améry's goal is to try to get behind mediated interpretations of suicide and understand those who take their lives "from the standpoint of their own world," as he writes, rather than from that of conventions practiced and observations made with other, more general, goals in mind.

Améry wrote frequently about people in extreme situations, their lives or their inner selves fundamentally threatened by illness, isolation, failure, or humiliation and degradation. Although he also wrote about political and social issues, his writings about people in extreme situations are not primarily political, seldom arguing for new legislation or social institutions to alleviate their condition. In *On Suicide* Améry rarely mentions anything like civil rights for suicides and attempted suicides. On one occasion, noting that "every progressive society" no longer considers gays to be sick or criminal—one wonders what societies Améry has in mind—he states that he doesn't "see why the suicidal should remain the last great outsiders." But even here, he is asking for understanding and for recognition of the humanity of their situation, rather than for giving them special status, socially or politically, as victims.

Just as *On Aging* deals with "a phase of changes and transitions, not a condition, not—age,"[1] *On Suicide* eschews the pursuit of the social conditions of suicide to concentrate instead on the internal evolutions that occur in the lives of people, real and imaginary, who want to end their lives voluntarily. Both essay collections also bear close affinities to three other books by Améry: *Lefeu oder Der Abbruch* (Lefeu, or the demolition), a cross between fiction and essay about a fictitious painter in Paris named Lefeu and his willful downfall; an unpublished novel written before World War II called *Die Schiffbrüchigen* (The shipwrecked); and a study of Flaubert's *Madame Bovary, Charles Bovary, Landarzt* (Charles Bovary, country doctor), a "portrait of a simple man" that concentrates on Emma Bovary's husband.[2] All five of these books are meditations on misfortune and failure, brought about by the threat of death, infirmity, personal unhappiness, or the impossibility of synchronizing one's individual existence with external conditions. In all cases, Améry seeks to throw light on an individual's state of mind on the basis of its particular situation, real or fictitious, without resorting to generalizations of morality, social science, or, in the case of Charles Bovary, literary convention.

Améry was born in Vienna in 1912 as Hans Maier. Early efforts to become a successful writer ended in failure. Because he was Jewish, he fled from the Nazis in Austria to

Belgium in 1938. Eventually arrested for resistance activities, he was tortured and sent to Auschwitz. He managed to survive Auschwitz and other concentration camps, then returned to Brussels after World War II and began writing, still in German, under the pseudonym of Jean Améry. *At the Mind's Limits*, his collection of radio talks about his experiences in the Holocaust, was published in German in 1966. This book made him famous in the German-speaking world. In spite of this success, he attempted suicide in 1974. He tried again in 1978 and succeeded.

Améry first thought of writing a "Meditation on Suicide" in the early part of 1975, thinking of it as a companion piece to *Lefeu* and *On Aging*. It would be a book that described suicide "from within," as he wrote in a letter, "so that the author completely enters into the closed world of the suicide. Therefore: nothing sociological, nothing psychological in the more narrow sense."[3] Further, he approached the subject in a literary manner and, consistent with his other writings, used frequent references and examples from poetry, theater, and fiction. He drew on philosophical literature as well and, to some extent, its methods, moving back and forth between the existentialism of Sartre and analytic approaches of positivism and linguistic analysis. Améry's use of these diverse, often contradictory, schools of philosophy was not intended to dazzle or prove something about philosophy as much as it was an attempt to cope with the difficult subject matter of suicide. He is hesitant and uneasy in his approach to the subject, apologizes for his digressions, and warns the reader that he is trying to deal with and describe things that are not accessible to language except by allusion and suggestion.

In 1793, Georg Christoph Lichtenberg wrote that attempts of one person to argue against another's suicide are useless. The only arguments that work, he maintained, are those that one has found for oneself and are "the fruit and result of our whole store of knowledge and of our acquired being. Thus everything calls out to us: strive daily after truth, learn to know the world, pursue the friendship of worthy men; then you will act always as is best for you. And if one day you find that suicide is the best step to take, if (in other words) all your arguments are not adequate to keep you from it, then that too is for you permissible."[4] This notion of Lichtenberg's—who, by the way, never tried to kill himself—about the uselessness of finding a common language to argue and communicate about the subjective and idiosyncratic reasons for committing suicide is similar to Améry's. "Voluntary death," he wrote in 1975, "is and always has been an *extraordinary act* that goes beyond the customary ordering of individual and social existence; this it has been even in circumstances where it has been socially accepted as a duty of honor (hari-kari) or as an obligation of taste (Petronius) or even as an order in the name of an unwritten officer's code (Lieutenant Gustl)."[5] Not only that, but one's basic self, Améry argued, is submerged under a fabricated ego that is merely the result of "formations and deformations brought about by the medium of society,"[6] a further potential source of distortion. For Améry, in agreement with Lichtenberg, the alienations and setbacks one experiences in one's life could lead to legitimate reasons for choosing a voluntary death, regardless of whether those reasons can be communicated. Hence, the difficulty of trying to understand why someone commits suicide. One is trying to

understand reasons expressed in a language that is individu-
ally subjective and not persuasive in the language of everyday life. Yet the individual situation, not the social situation, of each suicide's argument is, according to Améry, what
must be understood in order to understand why anyone
would choose to end one's life. Much of *On Suicide* is an
attempt to demonstrate the reasonable and permissible nature of choosing a voluntary death from the point of view
from which the choice is made and to understand it on its
own terms.

In *On Suicide*, Améry expresses his distrust for experts
and specialists such as physicians, psychologists, and soci-
ologists. This distrust is consistent with his other writings.
For example, in an essay on Jean-Luc Godard, one of his
many writings on the cinema, he observed that what he
was writing could not compete with the work of specialists
in film theory and criticism. It was not his intention to write
for an academic audience, but instead for the average intelligent moviegoer. He lamented the fact that "the second in-
dustrial revolution had put into effect a class of technocrats
and specialists who live in a universe that is inaccessible to
lay people." Its resulting vocabulary of "management, mar-
keting, computers, human engineering, and public relations"
was part of a development in which "serious questions of
life were either passé or the concerns of specialists."[7]

The essays of *On Suicide* explore the subject in a ram-
bling, frankly subjective, and openly hesitant effort to provide illumination, their aim being "not to make a bold description of the act," as Améry writes, "but rather to strive
for a gentle and cautious approach to it." One wouldn't have
to read Améry's Preface to recognize, in the book's meta-

phorical opening, that it is neither an academic study nor a journalistic survey. Améry often resorts to metaphor to describe his task. He uses literary examples to illustrate his arguments as much as he uses anecdotes from everyday experience. He uses examples from personal experience and personal acquaintance. These methods diminish the distance between him and his subject, giving the book a conversational, informal aspect, with even a few dashes of autobiography, even though Améry only occasionally indicates directly whether he is referring to himself or an imaginary person. Améry's style of argument has been described by Lothar Baier as a "doubting generosity" that seeks to avoid the attitude of one who is convinced he must be right. Baier connects this stance with Améry's "intimacy with literature" in general and with Thomas Mann in particular, noting that Améry's characterization of Mann's "gentle posture" in an essay written in 1975 to celebrate the hundredth anniversary of the novelist's birth can accurately be applied to Améry himself. The essay, "Bergwanderung" (mountain hike), is a key to Améry's approach to his subject matter. He admired Mann's language, whole paragraphs of which he knew by heart, because it seemed to be uncertain, "with its frequent adjectival couplings tending to the grotesque, with its timorously executed constructions: a discourse of the both-this-as-well-as-that." Améry found Mann's discourse to be one that is constantly open to doubt without falling into absolute relativity. He admired Mann's style for its acute awareness of sickness and death, of the vulnerability of human beings, and of the necessity to approach its subject matter with great care and discretion. By refusing to shut his emotions out of his thinking, Mann always wrote, according to

Améry, with a gentle regard for human behavior, using a language of skepticism and doubt and maintaining a consciousness that could not be reduced to social existence.[8]

Shortly after writing the essay on Thomas Mann, Améry reviewed Thomas Bernhard's *Breath: A Decision*, a memoir about the writer's extreme determination to live and overcome the threat of death when he was seriously ill. Stating that he does not believe in any kind of normative aesthetics, that his own aesthetics is "deeply skeptical," based entirely on his own subjective reception of a work of literature, Améry praised *Breath* primarily for its honesty, "perhaps the highest praise that can be given an author today."[9] These characteristics of Mann and Bernhard mark Améry's style and method: the "gentle posture," the language of doubt and skepticism without relativism, the inclusion of emotion in thinking, the urge to pursue problems outside of their social existence, and the attempt to be as honest as possible. Améry's somewhat old-fashioned style, one that uses words that are deliberately chosen for their qualities as archaisms and is rooted in the Enlightenment, aims to dig to the core of his subject without distorting it, without letting it become a virtuoso performance that could stand in the way of the reader's reception. Améry thought of himself as a reader, a nonprofessional reader, and he addressed the same kind of person—the kind of person most likely to be his listener when his words were first presented on the radio.

In trying to explain the special place of suicide beyond the limits of ordinary social life, Améry argues in the essays that follow that suicide contradicts "the logic of life." From the point of view of everyday life, killing oneself is pathological. But Améry denies that suicide is a sickness and rejects the use of pejorative words for it, such as the ordinary German word *Selbstmord* (self-murder), preferring to refer to it with the less frequently used *Freitod* (voluntary death). He argues that the internal psychic structure of each suicidal person is, in its full dimension, inaccessible to psychology, claiming that a comprehensive discourse on suicide has to begin where psychology leaves off. Furthermore, he insists that psychology belongs to the "logic of life," while suicide lies outside of this "logic."

Améry asserts that people kill themselves out of a sense of dignity, preferring annihilation to the continuation of an existence lived in ignominy, desperate pain (physical or mental), or utter helplessness. But he places the emphasis less on the pursuit of dignity than on choosing to live no longer in a wretched condition. To continue to live willingly in a miserable condition, to accept a life that one considers humiliating and worthless, is for Améry the greatest indignity. From this perspective he asserts that it is more "natural" to commit suicide than to wait for death to come. Now, it is obviously debatable whether a particular person's judgment about the worth of his or her life is not the result of a hysterical or severely depressed state of mind, a condition that could be improved by medical and psychological intervention, thus allowing the person to continue to live and perhaps even enjoy life and be happy. Améry is not comfortable with this therapeutic view, both because of his own experience when he attempted suicide in 1974, described in *On Suicide*, and because of his determination to recognize the legitimacy of choosing suicide and to assert that it is wrong to assume that all suicides are the result of an illness caused by depression or hysterics and to fail to recognize the value in an individual's own interpretation of his or her life, regardless of how dreary that interpretation may be.

Améry thought about death and suicide constantly, both in recalling his experiences in the German death camps, and in his preoccupation with aging and the deterioration of the body. He thought death was a meaningless nonentity, but he was also attracted to it. In an essay published in 1973, he describes a conversation with Elias Canetti and how impressed he was with the man's "extraordinary vitality," communicated both physically and verbally, especially when he said at one point, "I *hate* death." Améry describes how Canetti said it in a peculiar and personal way, "as if death were a somebody" against whom his hate could somehow have an effect. Améry says he listened attentively, because he, too, "who didn't hate death but instead anxiously longed for it," was also in his way dealing with the same subject. Later in the same essay he writes that he did not feel like living much longer.[10]

Whether Améry's longing for death resulted from his experiences in Auschwitz or not, it is hard to say. It seems that failure and suicide were significant features of his unpublished novel *Die Schiffbrüchigen*, written before World War II.[11] But the Holocaust must have augmented whatever preoccupation with these matters he had already formed and certainly contributed to his emphasis on the right of an individual to be free to choose to commit suicide. Auschwitz was a death factory, where dying was deliberately meted out to each inmate with the impersonal precision of an assembly line. People were killed with a determined policy that denied them even the most minimal consolation or recognition that they were human beings, let alone individuals. At the opposite pole to this is the extremely subjective act of an individual's voluntary death, an act through which, as Améry argues in *On Suicide*, one can truly attain self-realization. Death at Auschwitz was the most impersonal of deaths and the greatest denial of personal freedom, while death by suicide, as a voluntary death, a *Freitod*, was the most extreme affirmation of one's freedom and personal dignity. This is not to say that everyone who commits suicide does so in such a state of freedom or self-realization. Certainly, mass-hysterical suicides like the one at Jonestown cannot be called "voluntary deaths." Nor is this affirmation of the right to take one's life a recommendation to do so, as Améry clearly asserts. As is the case with many other forms of freedom, having the freedom to commit suicide doesn't mean that it has to be done or that it is always a good thing to do. Améry's final summation, at the end of *On Suicide*, makes it extremely clear that it is better to live a life of "smiling, breathing, and striding" than to kill oneself.[12] But those who can't live such lives should not be condemned and both their right to choose their destiny as well as the action they take, though horrifying, should be respected.

On Suicide has its cumbersome moments. Améry sometimes seems to be defensive or to want to explain things more than is necessary. His predisposition in this book toward poetic abstractions, anthropomorphic metaphor, and metaphysical pathos occasionally becomes irritating. But readers should look past these lapses. These essays present a perspective on suicide and individual freedom, on the humanity of those who are suicidal, which, without advocating the act, can illuminate much of what is thought about suicide as well as other aspects of the internal lives of human beings.

PREFACE

Those who know the books of the author, especially his study *On Aging*, of which the following reflections on the problem of voluntary death can serve as a direct continuation, do not need an orientation to what follows: they know that the volume before them cannot contain anything that in any way could suggest a work of social science.

But it is only fair to warn those for whom the author is an unknown. From these deliberations no one will gain the insights that that form of scientific research into suicide known as suicidology undertakes to present. Nor will readers learn anything about the country—and why specifically that one—in which more people kill themselves than in any other, nor will they read substantial information about the psychological and social processes (or pre-processes) that eventually lead to a voluntary death. No statistics will add to the volume of their knowledge, there are no graphic illustrations to make the results of scientific knowledge visible, nowhere does the author project a model of suicide.

This text is situated beyond psychology and sociology. It begins where scientific suicidology leaves off. Instead of viewing voluntary death from the outside, from the world of the living and surviving, I have tried to view it from the interior of those who call themselves suicidal or suicides. A "phenomenology of suicide?" That would be going a bit too far. I have dispensed with all concepts derived from the word *logos* and defined by disciplines of academic inquiry—out of modesty with respect to positive research. Also out of skepticism. Parts of the literature on the subject are known to me. But only as an exception have I here and there turned to this literature. Consequently, I have declined to provide a bibliography. At the same time it seems to me necessary to refer to the works and individuals to whom I owe the influences and knowledge without which what I have written could not have come into being. First of all there is Jean-Paul Sartre with his entire opus.[1] Even though the options I've made and the conclusions I've drawn are radically different from those of Sartre, I still turned to the massive edifice of his thinking when I was writing and needed intellectual support, and I feel constrained, even at this point, to speak emphatically about it. In addition, the lovely and profound book *La Mort* by Vladimir Jankélévitch, unbelievably not translated into German, has had an essential influence on the thoughts rendered here. Finally, there is one work of social science, quoted right in the first chapter and also after a long time still untranslated, to which I owe completely new insights into objective and scientific findings: the important book *Les Suicides* by Jean Baechler[2].

What is most essential, however, takes place in this volume beyond objective research. A rather long life of intimate association with death in general and with voluntary death in particular, conversations with knowledgeable friends, and certain life-determining individual experiences gave me the sense of my own legitimacy that is the precondition for writing. In many places readers might misunderstand me and think that I am conceiving here an apology for suicide. Such a misconception is to be emphatically precluded. What may appear to be apologetic is only my reaction to a kind of research that pursues the subject of suicide without being acquainted with the specific human beings in search of their own, freely chosen death—who find themselves in an absurd and paradoxical situation. I have tried to do nothing else than to pursue the insoluble contradictions of the *condition suicidaire* and to bear witness to them—as far as language can.

Brussels, February 1976   Jean Améry

On Suicide

I. Before the Leap

It's as if, to gain clarity, you are pushing open a very heavy wooden door that is creaking on its hinges and resisting your pressure. You apply all your strength, step across the threshold, and, after standing in a twilight gray, expect the light. Instead you are surrounded by a thoroughly impenetrable darkness. Distraught and fearful, you feel your way, touching objects here and there without being able to identify them. Eventually, your eyes very slowly grow accustomed to the dark. Uncertain contours appear; even your probing hands become more assured. Now you know that you're in that space that the German translation of the wonderful book *The Savage God* by A. Alvarez calls "the closed world of self-murder" (*Selbstmord*).[1] Self-murder? I don't like the word and will say why at the proper time. I prefer to speak of *voluntary death*, knowing well that the act itself is sometimes—frequently—brought into being by a condition of urgent compulsion. As a way of death, however, voluntary death is still freely chosen even when one is trapped in a vise of compulsions; there is no carcinoma that devours me, no infarction that fells me, no uremic crisis that takes away my breath. *I* am that which lays hands upon me, who dies after taking barbiturates "from hand to mouth."

The question of terminology needs to be clarified at the beginning, even if only in principle. In the course of the discussion we will no doubt let the casual nature of everyday language guide us and occasionally even speak of "self-murder" and quite certainly of suicide. *Sui caedere*: to kill oneself. —Remarkable how the latinized forms always suck the reality out of something. They can be handy, so I will use them for the sake of simplicity as soon as the reality I have in mind is sufficiently clear. Voluntary death becomes *suicide*, the persons who snuff themselves out become *suicides*, and *suicidals* or *potential suicides* are those who carry the project of choosing to die within them, regardless of whether they are seriously considering it or playing with it.[2]

But we aren't that far yet. We have only just now pushed the door open with great difficulty and halfway settled ourselves into a darkness that can never be completely illuminated—why it can't be is still to be told. But haven't flares been ignited everywhere? Isn't there psychology to help us? Sociology to orient us? Isn't there already a branch of research that calls itself suicidology to which we owe significant works of research? Of course. They are not unknown to me. I have plowed through many of them. I have learned this and that from these energetic compilations: how, where, and why people revoke themselves; which ages are most at risk; in which countries more and in which countries fewer voluntary deaths are recorded. By the way, the statistics of-

ten contradict one another, giving the suicidologists opportunity for scholarly argument. But I have also heard of some
concepts. Such as "short-circuit suicide." Well put. Or "narcissistic crisis." Also not bad. Or "act of revenge." *"Je me tue
parce que vous ne m'avez pas aimé . . . Je laisserai sur vous une
tache indélébile,"* (I am killing myself because you have not
loved me . . . I will leave an indelible stain upon you) as
Drieu la Rochelle[3] formulated it, a writer who eventually
killed himself, not because of a recalcitrant woman he wor-
shiped but from fear of the avengers of the Résistance. But
how simple all that is: you need only to follow and pay
attention to the professional literature and then you know—
what? Nothing. Whenever suicide is observed as an objective fact, as when scientists observe galaxies and elemental
particles, observers become distant from voluntary death,
more and more so in proportion to the data and facts they
gather. Their categories, scientifically serviceable, perhaps
even therapeutically useful—but just what does therapy
mean here?—are vehicles that, in a constantly accelerating
tempo, tear observers out of the magic sphere of the "closed
world." Ultimately, their distance is only measurable in light
years.

In his instructive little book *Le Suicide*, the French soci-
ologist Pierre Moron quotes the work of a colleague who
says, "The thought of suicide, a simple mental representa-
tion of the act, has to be theoretically excluded from a study
about suicidal behavior which, by definition, only begins
with the gesture. But when this is observed as the virtuality
of the act, one can find in the thought the same instinctual-
affective impulse that is in the act: the intention of giving
death to oneself." Now that's what I call sharp thinking.

Nothing can escape that man. But let's bring 23-year-old Otto Weininger[4] to mind now, a man who is full of himself and in whose brain, agitated to death, only *woman* is reflected again and again, the creature whom he despises yet for whom he is not able to master his desire; Otto Weininger, who constantly sees only the *Jew*, the most disgraceful and lowest of all creatures, the Jew that he himself is. Perhaps for him it was like being in a small room whose walls are moving closer and closer together. Moreover, his head is growing larger, like a balloon being blown up, and at the same time it is getting thinner. His head beats against all four walls as they relentlessly move closer. Every contact is painful and reverberates like the beat of a kettledrum. Finally, Weininger's skull, running in all directions, beats a raging drumroll—until it . . . Until it leaps into pieces or "goes through the wall," as those observing him outside the room are wont to say. That doesn't concern him any more. And what the skillful gentleman from France has to say could have concerned him even less. Weininger knew nothing of a "suicidal behavior." But I think, admittedly speculating, that he only saw and heard, without interruption, but with all the force of a heart trying to pull itself together, woman, Jew, ego: away with them all.

—Are we ready to find our way around in this darkness we've stepped into? I think so, because we have already given up trying to dissect what has thus been designated as "suicidal behavior," as if we were forensic surgeons with a piece of dead tissue. We are already on our way, *not away* from persons annihilating themselves, but *toward* them. They will thank us, without pleasure, insofar as chance permits that they survive. And if they don't thank us, then we are not necessarily completely wrong: it might be instead that friend X, who survived his attempt, has abandoned himself, having been called back, and is now compliantly and shamefully submitting to *the logic of life*, out of whose armor he had already broken.

Immediately, the pumped-up common sense that cannot see beyond its own interests will interpose here: Weininger? Why talk about someone like him as an example? And doesn't it sound like the self-importance of intellectual arrogance to drag him in? Psychologically there are completely different forms of "suicidal behavior" conditioned by many different kinds of causes, thoroughly difficult to unravel. No one is really qualified to speak of these forms except an expert on auto-aggression, on the Oedipus complex, on "social isolation," on narcissistic neurosis, on epileptic disposition, on hysterical theatricality, in short, an expert armed with psychosociological instrumentation! Why conjure up right at the beginning a myth of intellectual history such as Otto Weininger, a prime example of Jewish self-hatred, and, in an act of oversimplification, present his particular act as a metaphor? I know. Honor for those who deserve honor, and science fills me with so much respect that I would never dare . . . Yes, respect. But also a little contempt. Then further. There are forms and stories of development. There are ideas of voluntary death that are so different from each other that it seems only possible to say that their commonality consists in nothing other than the fact that a suicidal person is seeking a voluntary death.

Let's remain at first only with those who sought and found, the suicides, and let's raise the question whether in reality something else united them other than the objectively verified fact that they were putting an end to their life. We shall see. It is undeniable that there are acts of suicide that, at first glance, have hardly anything to do with each other as far as their causality, their transsuicidal intentions, and even their *ranking* are concerned. A report occurs to me that went through the Austrian press when I was young: a housemaid had thrown herself out of a window "because of her unhappy love for a radio lover," as it was expressed in the newspaper language of the time. How is one supposed to make this act agree with other, obviously quite incommensurable death wishes and ways of finding death? At an advanced age, P. F.,[5] a psychoanalyst and first-generation disciple of Freud, shot himself. Shortly before that he had lost the woman who had been his companion; moreover he was suffering from an inoperable cancer of the prostate. It was understandable when he reached for his revolver, even if it was noted, in an undertone with a serious expression, that it could not be condoned. In a great and rich productive life, the man had lived, learned, and accomplished much. There was nothing left to come his way except bodily pain and loneliness: what we call a future was blocked. And so he turned a nonfuture, which would have meant a life entirely enveloped in death, into something clear, into death itself. Or take Sigmund Freud. The old man's cancer of the gums was in its final stage. The patient's mouth produced a pestilential odor so obnoxious that his favorite dog wouldn't go near him anymore. He said to his personal physician that everything was just torture and more torture and demanded the injection that would liberate him—which his old friend did not deny him. That, too, is a clear case of socially accepted and recognized voluntary death. But what about Cesare Pavese, who killed himself at the height of his fame and powers as a writer because of an "insignificant love affair?" Or Paul Celan, *L'Inconnu de la Seine* (the unknown person found in the Seine), or Peter Szondi, the unknown person found in a Berlin lake, both of whom found quenching waters better than a life of honor and renown?[6] Do Pavese, Celan, and Szondi have more in common with the defenestrated housemaid from Vienna than with Freud and P.F.? And what about Schnitzler's Lt. Gustl, an invented but thoroughly true-to-life figure? He spent a night in the Prater, convinced that he had to kill himself because of an argument during which a master baker, superior to him in physical strength, had kept him from drawing his saber as required by the code of honor of the imperial and royal army.[7] He could have said to himself, "Fine, the fellow was stronger than I am and that's not my fault; and now if he is so crude as to let the disgraceful story get out and my superiors are dumb enough to expel me from the army, then I don't have to worry about it anymore; I'll take my own farewell and go into some sort of civil service." But the Kaiser's uniform was to him just as much a compulsory condition of all existence as the love of the singer with the melting voice was to the housemaid. Without this uniform he would—could—no more live than the girl could live without the love of the man who sang so tenderly "Two Fairy-Tale Eyes, as Lovely as the Stars"—and he only failed to shoot himself because, even before he took up his weapon, he learned by chance that the poor strong-armed baker had died that same night from a heart attack. Lt. Gustl and the housemaid stood under laws of a life worth living that were different from those of Freud, Federn,

Pavese, and Celan; laws they could not obey under the given circumstances.

This does not invalidate the judgments of suicidology, which would speak of Lt. Gustl's compelling obligation to an inhuman code of honor, of the triggering factor—the unhappy love—that simply brought the basic displeasure with life deep within the housemaid to a suicidal explosion, and perhaps of endogenous depressions in the cases of Celan and Szondi. Suicidology is right. Except that for suicides and potential suicides what it says is empty. For what it comes to for them is the total and unmistakable singularity of their situation, the *situation vécue*, (lived situation) that can never be completely communicated, so that therefore every time someone dies by his or her own hand or even just tries to die, a veil falls that no one can lift again, which in the best of cases can only be illuminated sharply enough for the eye to recognize as a fleeting image. We have yet to speak of such images. But before we get there, we need to ask about what our examples have in common beyond the objective facts that voluntary death occurred or seemed unavoidable. The answer can be given easily. It sounds trivial at first hearing; with a more thorough analysis it opens the abyss of the riddle of life. I am speaking of the *situation before the leap*.

Regardless of psychological motivation and the psyche's causal associations at the end of which the indescribable act stands, this situation before the leap is fundamentally the same in all cases. Suicides or potential suicides—for here it is not a matter of whether death has occurred or not—beat with their heads a raging drum tattoo against the advancing walls and eventually break through the barrier with a skull beaten thin and already wounded. One may have planned one's death in great serenity as a "balance suicide," as the relevant research on the subject describes it; another, under the precipitous pressure of an unbearable external situation, may have been driven to what is called a "short-circuit suicide"; still another may have been dosing suicidally through life for a long time in a condition of mourning and melancholy or, on the contrary, may have been, according to witnesses, in a good mood just a few hours beforehand— the moment before the leap makes all distinctions irrelevant and brings about a bizarre equality. Differences are always important to relatives or even to science. The latter, for instance, when dealing with the case of our housemaid, speaks of "insignificant motives." What does it know? Everything that can be known from outside, that is, nothing. I knew a man who took a good number of sleeping pills because of a marital squabble, was "rescued" by pure chance, lay in a coma for twenty-four hours, and still lives today. He was dragged to a neurologist who was a friend of his and who wisely said, "Don't you realize that things like domestic quarrels, tears, and reconciliations belong to vaudeville?" A trifle had escaped the doctor: what is to be called vaudeville and what is to be called tragedy is decided by the author.

Along with all other distinctions, the situation before the leap, that sometimes lasts only a moment, but at other times drags on for torturous hours, also obliterates the distinction of status: in that case the housemaid makes just as much of a heroic or heartrending figure as a great poet or a famous psychologist. This apparently simple person who jumped out of her window many decades ago won't get out of my mind. How did it begin? With "Two Fairy-Tale Eyes, as Lovely as the Stars," tenderly sung into her earphones as she sat alone on the edge of her little bed, softly sounding his words to herself. Impossible to think of her will resisting this tender lure. Perhaps she had written the heart-melting voice via the radio station and received no answer. Maybe she found a photo of the artist in some kind of stationery store, showing a man with smooth and oily black hair clinging to his head, soft cheeks, sweetly smiling at nothing. She loves, is not loved in return, she can't go on just by listening to him. If the arms of the man in the tuxedo are not going to embrace her then her world will be a world of torture and madness. Whomever she speaks to about it—the girl on the next staircase, the butcher boy—it's all the same: no one listens. She says, "I can't go on." Sigmund Freud said, "It's just torture and more torture." They find themselves before the leap—and at this point I hope no one dares to smile ironically or offer a learned word. This I do not tolerate, no matter how brilliant one is proven to be by one's sociological publications. Only those who have entered into the darkness can have a say in this matter. They'll unearth nothing that appears useful in the light outside. What they have brought from the depths will run like fine sand through their fingers by day. But that they, and only they, were on the right path, the way corresponding to the experience, will be confirmed by all who are suicidal, as long as they stick to themselves and do not deny themselves. It's nice to assume that the housemaid or Pavese or Celan would have been saved and taken into therapy, that all three would have unanimously proclaimed they had only been deranged for a moment, and that now everything is fine. Forgiven and forgotten. Now they would be filled with thanks for the hands that saved them and the generous words of enlightenment. Friends, life is still beautiful. But what does this prove? Really just the fact that, after successful therapy, they are *different* people, but not that they became better and more respectable ones. Here is the place, I think, to put a stop to temporality and historicity.

Jean Barois, the title character of the novel by Roger Martin du Gard, wrote in his last will and testament when he was 40 years old that he did not want a Christian burial because at that time, in full possession of his moral and intellectual powers, he was a declared atheist and what he might say or do later, with a diminished constitution, should not be valid. Jean Barois, as an old and sick man, had the pastor come at the hour of his death. Now *who* was the real Jean Barois? If we side with temporality and historicity, then logically Jean Barois has to be the dying old man who asked for the priest because all preceding moments of life would have been stratified in him and in their stratification would have permeated one another, every later one assimilating the earlier ones and thereby transforming them. —I am not going to say decidedly that this is not so, no matter how much my personal sympathy belongs to the 40-year-old still in his full powers. But I'm refraining from this personal inclination of mine and only want it kept in mind that every temporal section of our existence, in fact even every moment, has its own logic and its own sense of honor, that the temporal process of maturing is also at the same time a process of dying and that therefore, later in her life, my poor housemaid would possibly never have reached the same grade of authenticity as she did when she jumped out the window. Did her great love ennoble her? Nonsense. It only fulfilled her completely, bestowing to her existence a density that scarcely would have been granted to her later with a good husband and in the midst of happy children. She was living at the utmost and, therefore, the truest degree at the moment of jumping.

We'll speak of this again and again, for it is the alpha and omega of the problem. What happens here is obvious. Death, with which we have to live in any case as soon as we get older, which grows in us and makes itself felt as *angor* (anguish) or threatens us from outside as terror, death is seized upon here. The phrase *seized upon*, as if it sounded like something else, has the same metaphorically twilight characteristic as when we say that we *flee* into death. Where do we flee? Nowhere. We begin a trip in order to arrive at a point we can't imagine. And what do we seize upon? The word fails, must fail, because "death is nothing, a nothing, a negativity," as I have written elsewhere (in *On Aging*). Still, whether to "flee" into a region that does not exist or to seize upon something that has no being and therefore is not the "nothing" (which has always seemed to me to be a sloppy form of expression) but simply "not," are two different kinds of things. Waiting for death is just a kind of passive action, insofar as this paradox, imposed upon me by grammar, is allowed. But voluntary death, the killing of oneself, is without a doubt an activity not only in grammar but also in fact. Thus, living-on-to-death and the autonomous act of suicide cannot easily be compared, regardless of whether the result in both cases is the same. People who must die are in the condition of answering a destiny and their rejoinder consists of fear and bravery. But suicides or potential suicides speak themselves. They speak the first word. They cannot ask, "Death, where is thy sting?" after they have been addressed by death itself in whatever form (sickness, danger, or simply a decrease in vitality). But the suicide is the one that calls—and it is death that imparts the incomprehensible, inaudible answer. That means that a suicide gets right up from the "mattress sepulcher" on which he is lying and strikes.[8] Walls that have moved closer, that's one thing; but *La tête contre les murs* (The head against the walls), the title of a novel by Hervé Bazin, that's something else entirely. Anyone who wants to commit suicide is breaking out, out of the logic of life, as I've already indicated. This logic is given to us, the biologist knows it just as well as the behavioral scientist, and perhaps also the physicist, because recent works of theoretical physics seem to allow the conclusion (one that of course lies beyond the older vitalism) that *bios* and human being are perhaps more than "chance hits," as Jacques Monod thought. The logic of life is prescribed for us, or "programmed," if you wish, in every daily reaction. It has gone into our daily language. "In the long run, you've got to live," people say, excusing every miserable thing they have initiated. But *do you have to live*? Do you always have to be there just because you were there once? In the moment before the leap, suicides tear to pieces a prescription of nature and throw it at the feet of the invisible prescriber, just like a statesman in the theater who throws a contract, which from that moment is just a piece of paper, at the feet of another statesman. Even before any questions are asked, those ready to kill themselves shrilly scream, "No!" Or they numbly say, "Maybe someone has to, but not me, and I'm not going to bow down to an ardent compulsion that comes from somewhere outside as a law of society and from within as a *lex naturae*, and which I don't want to recognize anymore."

This is where they all find themselves, the Kleists,

Chattertons,[9] Paveses, Celans, and Szondis and all those innumerable ones without a name who by their deed, whether
their plan "succeeds" or not, give expression to something
deeply mysterious and logically contradictory. I mean
Schiller's proposition, "Life is not the highest good of all."[10]
According to reason, this saying comes out badly, even if
one overlooks the fact that the person who coined it wrote
it down without much previous reflection, and merely for
an assured theatrical effect. For what is it supposed to mean?
There can only be goods in life, not in the negative nonentity of death; and therefore life must be the first, last, deepest, and highest of such goods. But for anyone standing before the leap, the judgment contained in Schiller's line,
absurd and to be rejected by rigorous logic, contains good
sense, a sense that is of course already beyond life and its
logic; beyond all reason (which is only life's subservient
spirit), beyond everything that even the most thorough researcher in the field of suicidology is capable of bringing
forth.

Two examples come to mind again, both closer to my
sensibility than the great suicides and suicidal figures of
world and intellectual history, nearer than Empedocles or
Demosthenes or Cato or the Buddhist monks who set themselves on fire as offerings to liberation or Stefan Zweig or
Montherlant:[11] Lt. Gustl and the housemaid. According to
Gustl, the Kaiser's uniform he wears is worth more than
life—a contradiction because this piece of clothing can only
be worn by the living. To the housemaid the unctuous man
with his sweet song and two fairy-tale eyes counts more
than existence, an absolute contradiction since there is no
tuxedo-bewitchment and tender voice beyond life. Thus it

was an absurd act that the maid committed; it was absurd behavior for Lt. Gustl to spend the night in the Prater, knowing that at the crack of dawn in his bare room at the army base he would take his revolver and shoot a bullet into his temple.

I am only asking my readers to be ready to understand. I am not thinking specifically of the absurdity of the psychological reasons—either the royal and imperial officer's code or the validation of the licorice-melting voice. The psychic constitution of Gustl and the maid is *also* absurd, that's obvious. People can live without a sword, they can also live without that male beauty that, under the light, may look just as lamentable as the singer Müller-Rosé, seen by the young Felix Krull in the dressing room putting on his make-up.[12] The absurdity I have in mind lies on a higher—higher or deeper, it's the speech we're accustomed to—, in any case, on a different plain from the psychological one. A suicide so urgently understandable, psychologically and socially, as that of the important psychoanalyst P.F. is, in the existential arena that I envision, no less absurd, for even it is a rejection of the logic of life. Or should I say, the logic of being? It doesn't really matter because in any case it is not possible to convey sufficiently with language things that *per definitionem* lie outside of language. However that may be, even the very sick, old psychologist, satiated with life and with a full spirit, hastened, armed with his pistol, toward the not. He was rid of bodily pain and of the grief for his already departed companion. But whoever is not is also exempt from no pain. In no way different from the maid, P.F. broke open the fetters of the logic of life and threw himself metaphorically on the breast of a not that in no way grants the soothing and sweet alleviations that everyone knows who has ever been given a euphoria-inducing injection of morphine.

I believe in all seriousness that the discourse on voluntary death only begins where psychology ends. Still, it is good to be dispassionate and not to sound important with words like "high" and "deep." In fact, I have to admit that the results of these considerations won't amount to anything for anyone who "stands in life still fresh and gay," as the song says. These thoughts basically concern only the suicidal or, to narrow the circle even more, only those who, from their point of view, are already standing on the threshold that will become their springboard into the abyss. Of course, because they have already long since moved beyond the smart-aleck, worldy-wise philosophy of life that "everyone has to live," this kind of feeling one's way in the dark, this kind of talk, moving forward with uncertainty and discussing what no longer can be discussed, may be the only thing that still concerns them. Think of Lt. Gustl from the point of view of a vitally reasonable man who says to him, "Good friend, there are so many civilians who live without the Kaiser's uniform; why do you imagine that you couldn't be like one of them?" The sun smiles on the clothes of civilians, too, women also love men without epaulets. Arthur Schnitzler, himself a man of reason, of life, of a cheerful but pessimistic enlightenment, was the author of another work, the play *Freiwild* (Fair game), which likewise deals with an officer who, on account of an absurd act of honor and dishonor, has to decide to kill himself. At that point a humane individual comes on the stage and advises his comrade to disarm since he is dealing with the wrong person, one who, after an argument about a woman, isn't interested in "satisfaction." But the officer says, "As what shall I continue to live, having once been Oberleutnant Karinski?" And the friend says, "Well, what is so great about being Oberleutnant Karinski?" In response to which Karinski says, "Everything, for me everything." The author clearly stands on the side of humane and urbane objections to this kind of thing, which he certainly viewed as "madness." Still, because he was not a psychologist, not a psychotherapist, but just the writer Arthur Schnitzler, he forces even the reader into Karinski's imperial officer's uniform so that we say to ourselves at the end, "Yes, what is the poor fellow really going to be after having once been Oberleutnant Karinski?"

Or take the Weininger case. Here let's consult with a psychotherapist, one of the gentle kind, I'd suggest, who has a direct connection to the Good Lord. And this one talks to Weininger as if he were talking to a sick horse, as one would say in Austria. "But my dear friend, in the first place, it's not true that the woman you desire and hate is a Lilith, destroying and defiling everything with that black bush between her lily-white thighs; second, the Jew that you are and can't bear to be is not at all the repulsive creature you claim to see; I can gladly give you one example after another that proves the exact opposite." Of course, the therapist, in making a logical effort, would not argue so primitively in practice and would rather "get right to the bottom" of things to reduce Weininger's self-hatred to absurdity. In the global system of *life* he would have inviolable justice on his side. But let's assume that Weininger, at the moment when these comforting words, so rich in illumination, reached him, was already standing on the threshold. In that case, such worldly wisdom would have amounted to nothing more than the ringing of a fool's bells. The officer in Schnitzler's *Freiwild* thought that being the Oberleutnant Karinski was everything. Weininger considered the Jew that he himself was to be a filthy scum that only death could wash away. The one as well as the other will turn away with disgust from anyone trying to offer consolation.

It cannot be emphasized enough that in spite of taking note of psychology here and there, we are outside of its realm with such considerations. Psychology is something for an expert. However, the act of leaping, no matter how full it may be of psychological impulses, can't be open to any further psychological insight because it breaks with the logic of life and therefore also with psychology. Let's take a breath together for a moment so that we can deal once again with this not entirely simple concept of the "logic of life" that we have set above psychology. It is just not enough simply to refer to facts about the preservation of the self and the species. For years, basic required reading on the fundamentals of logic have demonstrated conclusively, disregarding certain differences among the various camps of logicians, something that is, in my opinion, an irrefutable fact: the statements of logic are *empty*. They are, according to their nature, tautological; they are "analytic judgments," in Kant's terminology, or they are rules for the recasting of thoughts. They express nothing about reality or, to put it another way, they never impart anything new to the knowledge of this reality. Nevertheless, reality is always their basis. That something cannot at one time be and not be is a primal form of empirical knowledge we take from reality. If I therefore speak of a logic of life or a logic of being, then I mean that all logical conclusions that we draw in statements about life are constantly bound to the fact of this life. One can't say that in order to live well it is best not to live. That would be pure nonsense. In this way, the logic of what is incorporates the logic of society, the logic of behavior in general, the logic of everyday activity, and finally that formal logic that must exclude death. What Epicurus said and to which I will not tire of referring, remains valid: namely, that death does not concern us because as long as we are, it is not, and as soon as it appears, we are not any more. It remains not only valid, but empty in an almost humorous way. But more than empty and abysmally offensive for those who have to do with death, is the thought that even that has its logic. The *logic of death* is not a logic in the usual sense, upholding reason alone, for it allows no conclusion other than just one, again and again and again: not is the same as not, with which the statement of every logical (that is, analytic) judgment, already in itself containing no reality, loses its last tie to reality; that tie above all in which the equation of two categories of being that are symbolically recorded as in mathematics, or are rooted in everyday language, is now related to something that is nothing and is not—a pure negation, an accursed inconceivability.

Actually, someone standing before the leap—and in this alone it is important to me—has at the same time one foot still in the logic of life and the other in the anti-logical logic of death. Because we mean by the logic of life not only the immanent logic of behavior that preserves the self and the species, to which we are tributary, but also the logic gained from this logic as an abstraction of higher order, one that weighs being against being, sets one against the other, and therefore can come to the knowledge of the logical "true" and "false," whereby true as much as false are tacitly accepted as categories of being because there is no bridge from being to nonbeing—because of all this, we are so helpless in thinking about death. A person who leaps, however, is in the most real meaning of the word already halfway "on the other side," to speak metaphorically, and it doesn't matter whether on the empirical level this act leads to the end or leaves someone who's been "rescued" hanging in a vacuum. On the other side? This "other side" does not exist: those who leap carry out something indescribable and logically perverse; "*Le faux, c'est la mort,*" (Falsehood is death) as Sartre says. They are torn between the logic of life and the logic of death: in that consists the ontically murky singularity of their situation. They know the logic of death or the anti-logic of death, even if they have nothing to say about it, even if no room remains for them in the system of psychological concepts and expressions. How comparatively easy it is for suicide psychology, which either dissects those who are suicidal according to a terminologically unshakable method or, more favorably, approaches them with great care, on tiptoes, as it were. This is especially so because a rescued suicide has returned again to the logic of life and speaks its language to the satisfaction of those who belong to it and to society in general, thus illustrating the ideas we read in most studies about suicide. But those who have jumped have known nothing of death; they have confused it with conditions of life. Those who have gained their lives back again often say with embarrassment—for in our civilization suicide is something one is ashamed of, something like sickness, or better, like poverty—that they "wanted to have peace and quiet," as if death were a condition describable in categories of being rather than by the negating not. A contemporary suicide researcher informs us of a man wrenched from suicide who told how, after taking a considerable dose of sleeping pills, he made himself "quite comfortable in bed" and even "ate some chocolate." As the poet says, he had "given himself a little treat"; it was something to be glad about. But I hesitate to believe in this comfort. Hadn't he seen the mist of total negation rise up and spread itself around the room? (I, too, am guilty of using inadmissible metaphors, I know, but language, my only instrument of communication, leaves me no choice, only the torture of insufficiency.) But one thing seems incontestable to me, regardless of the metaphors: even those suicidal individuals who are looking for "peace" or "the depths of sleep" know in a region of their existence, for which the term "the unconscious" would be only a harmless euphemism, that they are not entering into sleep and peace, but instead are making a leap toward a something that is not anything—and much too horrible for one to lament. One could object that my propositions can be dismissed in cases in which the person about to leap is a believer: *that person* thinks—and this thinking would reach into the ultimate depths—that he or she is probably not entering into the sleep and peace of this world but probably is moving away toward something more beautiful and enticing: toward God.

I doubt it. At the proper time it will be necessary to speak more exactly about voluntary death and Christianity. For the time being, I will say only this in anticipation: for those who are really believers, the situation before the leap cannot arise, because voluntary death, "self-murder," to express it suitably in this connection, is a sin. But God is great, the limits of His mercy have not been set; for once He will forgive. So believers snatch death to their breast so that it might embrace them with the love of God. And then everything is good and all our problems of the logical confusion in life and death are only idle brooding.

It is *not* good, that is the calamity. For the civilization in which we live, the spirit of our times, if you will, is so constituted that only in an infinitely tiny minority of human beings—those who just let the Good Lord hold sway and do as He pleases—is faith so deeply anchored that in such hours it can be an existential certainty. But there are real people who hold sway as living persons and as potential suicides and don't give divine power and glory a chance. In principle when I start from a condition, a *vécu*, that is different from, and more than, the arid field cultivated only with the greatest trouble by psychology, the situation of those before the leap is always the same one, regardless of whether they call themselves believers or not. Lt. Gustl had been raised as a Catholic, just like every upright royal and imperial officer; his creator tells us not one single word about his God, before whom the young man was about to sin so severely. It is true that Schnitzler, in his best stories, stays within the framework of psychology. Mama, Papa, his hometown Graz, his little girlfriend, and his comrades on the parade ground. All the more reason to have introduced God into his story if it had seemed plausible to him that He played an important role in Lt. Gustl's world. "Who is Schnitzler, anyway?" I hear someone ask. And isn't psychology being misused here as a mystification for the sake of ontological game-playing? The physician and writer Arthur Schnitzler was not a proven psychologist; nevertheless, he was one of the few contemporary authors who rated Sigmund Freud very highly. He was not an anthropologist. But he understood something about human beings. Every line of his work testifies, irrefutably, to this. It is also true that he was a psychological writer and not a phenomenological thinker. Nevertheless and precisely *because* he was acquainted with human beings, we have an idea of the abyss of the riddle behind the inner monologue his young officer carries on a whole night long—a monologue which, by the way, is a good match for other more famous soliloquies. Who are we? Where do we come from? Where are we going? Schnitzler holds himself back modestly, lets his figures only say and think whatever people blabber and brood about in their unpracticed brains. He leaves the riddle open, but knows, however, that it pesters us; and so he is a witness, well equipped to express here even that which he does not want to express, even that which cannot be expressed.

This is an uncanny landscape I am entering when I try to substantiate this; a swampy area, a bog hung with mist, before which the essayist should protect himself. He doesn't; he's not accustomed to being concerned about himself. And so let's say right here and let's also offer a vulnerable flank to every kind of criticism: one can't get through this with clear thinking. In a much-quoted *Tractatus* it says, "To an answer that one cannot express, one cannot express the question as well." And, "What one cannot speak of, one must be silent about."[13]

This is valid and remains unshakable whenever we're dealing with intersubjectively binding judgments, when philosophy claims to be serving "science." It becomes invalid as soon as philosophy's unfulfilled claim to scientific method is surrendered and knowledge of what is not knowable, observed a priori as such, is subject to a paradoxical experiment. And a necessary one. For the neopositivism inspired by Ludwig Wittgenstein is always simultaneously right and wrong. It's right when it rejects false questions for the sake of scientific judgments, that is to say, judgments that only make sense in the field of the logic of life. It is wrong whenever one has to step beyond this field—and *the fact that* such intellectual deviations and offshoots are both unavoidable and imperative always stands out wherever and whenever reflective persons are concerned with the kernel of things. "The riddle does not exist," says the Wittgenstein of the *Tractatus,* and he of course means by that only that the mystery is a matter of mysticism, of "moonbeams by day." I don't agree. Mysticism doesn't produce anything but mystification and mystagogy. The riddle that not only exists but that penetrates all of our acts of being is again and again a matter of speech. Certainly, a kind of speech that is helpless and vulnerable and that every nincompoop can gratuitously make ridiculous; and one by which everyone, when standing before the abyss, must test and prove oneself. It is imperative to reflect upon this mystery, in talk that is circular—or, more exactly, half-circular—, repetitious, struggling constantly for precision though never attaining it. One *may* talk without clarity about that to which the light of clear language (*du langage clair*) does not shine. And the riddle exists.

Have I strayed away from my theme? But no, on the contrary, I have been approaching it steadily. For we don't know of any riddle that would be more distressing than death—and within that riddle, voluntary death, that increases and multiplies the general contradiction or absurdity of death into something immeasurable. Now Lt. Gustl can withdraw. We are concerned with more important things than with such a featherweight person. It is best to speak of X, an abstraction of the person taking the leap, more familiar to us even as a pale shadow than any concrete or materialized phenomenon can ever be. I am asked how I know this pattern. And I answer without hesitation: from introspection and empathy. What did Sartre know of Flaubert's first pseudo-epileptic attack? Nothing and everything. With an ability to surmise well, he approached the incident after studying the meager documents available to him—and look how this intuitive power endowed him with a capability to set associative mechanisms in motion, a capability that those who merely work hard to collect "material" do without. So, it is possible, if one is gifted in surmising, to pursue the voluntary death of X. In taking this approach, one will be permitted to say tentatively that the abstraction X and all its possible concrete manifestations were constantly standing in the shadow of death's absurdity, that this complex (X and its manifestations) brought the latter, death's absurdity, to a head, thereby intending to neutralize it in a climax, because its condition suggests the proposition that what is not permitted to be cannot be. This conclusion is as sharp as a knife, no doubt about it, and if the poet, who played a humorous trick on the riddle in his little verse, had not surrendered to mystagogy, he would have been quite the poetic thinker to help us here. Weininger could not bear to be a Jew: he was one. My housemaid could not bear to be an anonymous woman upon whom the singer's attention was never bestowed: she was one. Only death remained as a way out, a nonway, because it was leading nowhere. Weininger did not become a non-Jew by killing himself. The poor creature at the kitchen sink was not the radio lover's loved one and did not fall upon death into the performer's arms. Their suicides were therefore "senseless"—aren't they in every case?

Here I'll make a short pause for a word or two *ex domo* and *pro domo*. In my book *On Aging*, in which I ventured to take my first steps toward approaching the occurrence of death, I quoted Nietzsche: "Death is only a death that is not free under despised conditions, a death at the wrong time, a cowardly death. Out of love for life one ought to want death differently, free, conscious, without surprise," and I spiritedly added, "A fool's story of a voluntary death."—Since that was brought to press, eight years have passed; the spirit is no longer so bold. The stretch of time hasn't made me smarter, God knows! But it has brought something new to me, for time doesn't stop bringing things to maturity. So although I won't take back the phrase "fool's story," I will cut it down drastically by assigning it to the realm of the logic of life. But here we are dealing with a logic that never fully intends to release itself from itself—that is, from life— but that still, with a tiny and uncertain step, goes beyond itself, away toward the anti-logic of death. So that I can say and want to say: With their absurd act, those who have chosen a voluntary death—X the abstraction, the housemaid, Celan, Kleist, Hasenclever, Hemingway, whoever:[14]— have not only provided the deadly incontestable evidence that life is not "the highest good of all," have not only pointed out to us that the phrase "What must not be cannot be" is more than a pensive joke, but they have resolved death's contradiction (living-dying), though at the price of another and more horrifying contradiction, which could be called: *I die, therefore I am.* Or: I die, therefore, life and everything there is as far as judgments are concerned has no value. Or again: I die, therefore I *was,* at least in a foolish way in the moment before the leap, what I could not be because reality would not allow it to me: Weininger as a non-Jew, the girl with the broom as the sweetheart of the singer.

Someone might wonder whether what I have been trying to say and am about to say is logically a demonstrable piece of nonsense and empirically not true. If so, then I've talked absurd rubbish, put words together *sans rime ni raison.* Thank you very much for the lucid correction. But I know a trifle I can add, one that escaped my censors: that when I took the daring step to add this manifest absurdity, I did so because we must have the courage to take that step if we want to approach the riddle *without* outlining a shabbily structured and barely existing metaphysics, nourished only by concepts that are not based on perception. By doing this, am I opposing reason and protecting people who are suicidal? Childish objection. Reason is not reason when it is not *more* than reason. And I haven't the least intention of calling people to action: Now please kill yourselves at will, and your voluntary death will bring you intellectual honors. If it could be so simple, I would remain silent. But as I am speaking, I am only getting ready for the terrain, as good or bad as it may be, the misty bogs upon which we have to continue to move if we want to bring more to light than a few pieces of data and a few trivialities.

Let's recapitulate the results of this laborious work so

far. We differentiated our thinking from all formulations of suicidology located in the realm of positive scientific method. We established that logic is always the logic of life and that suicide, the "act that no words describe, that breaks all bonds" (Golo Mann in his memoir of his brother Klaus),[15] also bursts the fetters of pure and practical reason. In addition: that in contradiction to Golo Mann's resignation, the aim here is certainly not to make a bold description of the act but rather to strive for a gentle and cautious approach to it, done of course with a loss of logical stringency and with the help of a doubtful use of metaphor. Finally: that such a process can be justified by the wary urgency to speak of just that "riddle," supposedly indiscussable, in the face of the threat of dullness on the one hand, blind madness on the other. We have taken up a question that, in the sense of modern logic, is an over-and-done-with "sham question." This we have done in order to demonstrate that it is not such a sham, rather that it plagues what are perhaps the deepest levels of our existence, by which fact alone a treatise on the question is justified. Here we enter into an obligation none other than this: that under certain impossible conditions it is necessary to think "toward" things that are doubly unthinkable—just as when one begins to think or be concerned about anything, one moves mentally in that direction—and that, in proceeding, something unthinkable can be represented as something partly thinkable.

I'd like to have a contract with my readers that they won't need to countersign because it has to be left to them whether or not they want to be affected by the absurdity (which is certainly not the author's invention or even a trick of his, but is the most extreme ignominy of the *condition humaine*), and by the paradox and the contradiction; that they can step aside at any time into healthy human understanding. They will be more inclined to this when they are trying to deal with something that is, as I've said, doubly unthinkable: with the *death* that everyone dies and that everyone experiences more or less consciously as a primal contradiction; but beyond that, with *voluntary death*. This act tries to cancel the primal contradiction, something it cannot succeed in doing. Suicides plunge into the abyss of an even deeper contradiction by not only dying (or preparing to die), but *by de-selfing their self themselves*.

The suicidal experience this in the situation before the leap, more or less consciously, with higher or lower insight, in serenity or exaltation, hysterically and theatrically, or moderating themselves with discipline. Jew, woman, ego, thinks Otto Weininger or he doesn't think it and is merely embraced and crushed to pieces by the three notions. Without the two fairy-tale eyes I do not want to live, my girl thinks or doesn't think at all, only senses something that we metaphorically describe as an unendurable "pressure." The Kaiser's uniform: this notion penetrates Lt. Gustl: even though in the long stretches of time during a night that is supposed to be his last it never happens that these words are thought out in him, it is thought without language. Here the limits of my language are no longer the limits of my world:[16] but fencing in the latter posits what is off limits to language. Being has a logical syntax that is difficult to research because it carries its contradiction—not being—inside itself. And when someone forcibly brings up this not being, that is, this syntactical impossibility, that someone becomes a person of nonsense. Nonsense, not deluded sense.

Those who leap have not necessarily fallen into delusion, they are not even "disturbed" or "deranged" in all circumstances. The inclination to voluntary death is not a sickness of which one has to be cured as one is cured of measles. —But about that later. Our eyes have only just accustomed themselves partly to the darkness. We have to stare with the eye of a nocturnal bird.

II. How Natural Is Death?

A young man, rewarded by his father with a handsome sports car because he excelled in passing his examination, took his first lengthy motor trip and, through carelessness— he apparently took a poorly judged corner too quickly— was killed before his time. As everyone would say, this was a highly unnatural, even scandalous, death. This young man was not just the student he'd been as he lay there on the hot pavement, breathing his last in convulsive agony. He was, in an embryonic stage, perhaps a brilliant lawyer, a much sought-after physician, a renowned architect. In the world's opinion, he was the father of a family who would no longer raise his children, make his wife happy and unhappy, or go to parties and the theater. One finds some of the best words against the unnaturalness of the violent death of a young person in a famous poem by C. F. Meyer: "The wreaths, granted to you if you had lived, not attained."[1]— Somewhere else, an old man died at the age of 90 years. He passed away gently. His powers had slackened and his memory refused to serve; in the end he sat all day long, just drowsing in his armchair, where they eventually found him dead. And there was probably no one, even among his closest relatives, who could be heard vehemently protesting. The man died a natural death, that is clear.

Between these two extreme examples, however, there extends a whole scale of others that cause us to have doubts about the distinctions among natural death, unnatural death, and even the kind of death that is against nature. At 36 years, at the peak of his fame and glory, the angelically beautiful, singularly spiritual actor Gérard Philipe died; his widow, Mme. Anne Philipe wrote a moving book about this death, *Le temps d'un soupir* (The time of a sigh). As a 23-year-old, the nineteenth-century German writer Georg Büchner was snatched away by a "putrid fever," as a penetrating metaphor puts it in bringing the horrifying facts of the case to our consciousness. Concerning the early death of Joachim Ziemssen, who, "a soldier, and brave," departed this life as a victim of laryngeal tuberculosis, his creator Thomas Mann says, "He looked at the ground, as though observing the earth. It was so odd: he walked here, in a proper and orderly manner, he greeted passers-by in his courtly way, kept to his external appearance and *bienséance* as always—and belonged to the earth. Well, we all belong to it, sooner or later. But to belong to it in such a short time, so young and with such a good, cheerful determination to serving the colors, that is bitter . . ."² One does not have to be a flag-waver or as young as Lt. Ziemssen for death to appear as something contrary and a provocation to an intemperate rebuttal. It was not "natural" that Schiller died at 46. If Kafka was mowed down at 41, the literary conscience of the world bristles at such a disgraceful triumph of a nature that knows nothing of itself, just as we know so little of it, in spite of all our scientific insights. Not everyone is Gérard Philipe, Büchner, or Kafka. Then there was the professor of mathematics I once knew who, at 46 years old, in the passage of one day to another, succumbed to a stroke. Again, I also heard of a successful businessman, in his fifty-fifth year of life, who could not stand up to the "stress" everyone talks about and died of a heart attack. If the philosopher Ernst Bloch, like his colleague Adorno, had gone to his death at 66, one would apparently only think of him incidentally as a state thinker of the East German government.[3] Adorno's death was hardly less "unnatural" than the passing of Georg Büchner. Here as much as there, the continuity of a creative existence was chopped to pieces so that in both cases we tend to object, like Voltaire, who protested against the earthquake of Lisbon in the name of the mind. Basically, death is never natural, especially not for people who are threatened, insofar as they are only halfway in control of their senses. A few years ago, it happened that I helped nurse a 94-year-old, still very lucid neighbor into death. This emaciated man sat upright in his bed, tried to catch his breath, and said, "These are my last days." He did not say it in agreement with his moribund constitution, and as he felt a deceptive relief for a few hours, he urgently demanded his favorite meal, brussels sprouts.

Looked at in the light, the whole question of the naturalness or unnaturalness of death often seems to be just one of semantics. Here, everyday language and logical discourse are no longer united. Death is *in every way natural* insofar as we derive this word from "nature" and understand "nature" to mean the total causal events that make up the outside world and are, with respect to our ego, the masters of our existence. Viewed this way, it is obvious that for our ego (a psychic and intellectual phenomenon, even if to my mind it means only a "bundle of feelings"), even our kidneys, our stomach, our heart, the treasured heart of metaphor, are only parts of the outside world. On the other hand, everyday language, even if conceptually unclean, functions communicatively as a social network upon which our life depends. In this it is once again more intelligent than the rigor of linguistic philosophy is inclined to think. In its vagueness and ambiguity, it constantly starts with facts that can be captured statistically and takes these as norms. Everyday language does not speak of "natural" as though it were taking the word back to the concept of nature, but means instead what it considers to be "normal," that is, what for a particular population at a particular time becomes quantitatively the norm. —I am inclined to speak here of "natural" and "unnatural" death at once in the sense of everyday language and semantic tidiness, because we cannot do without one or the other if we want to be understood. This practice, highly dubious as it is and above all indifferent to every methodological order, will cause everything I bring forth to stand in a twilight conducive to optical deceptions, in the twilight of the reality in which we move.

If I say therefore that for a dying person who is lucid death appears everywhere and at all times as unnatural, then with this expression I am situated somewhere between everyday language and a language of logical clarity. To the world, which is mediated to us through everyday language, every death, after the first shock has subsided and time's cicatrizing silent work of acclimatization has taken place, is in the end "normal" or "natural." Gérard Philipe died at 36: what a scandal. All right, he died unfortunately at 36: a definite percentage of people are still dying in France at this age even today and we can leave it at that—after the indignant outrage, the insight into necessity, that is, the *lack of freedom* in speech thrown into chains by reality. X has wretchedly come to his end before his time on some highway? People take umbrage, express resistance at first. And afterwards comes something that calls itself experience: that's just the way it is, every year so-and-so many people have fatal accidents on the streets and he was one of them; how sad, but ultimately how normal, how natural. And Y killed himself? Unheard of, unacceptable incident, unbearable for the sympathetic heart. Later: Y went to his death by his own hand; suicides exist and he was one of them. Mourning decreases with time, one can't live with the dead. In a mysterious way everyday language approaches again to be the semantically and logically more genuine language. To die naturally becomes what alone can be defined in logical language as dying "through nature" or through intersubjectively observable courses of causal events in space and time which *à la longue* (in the long run) only a crazy person doesn't recognize.

For a person getting close to death it is of course different. Objective circumstances do not concern him at all. We can be sure he doesn't feel the deposits of matter in his coronary vessels, but he does have "pressure in the chest," which only *he* recognizes and about which the others, including his physician, know nothing. Although he can intellectually step out of his ego by believing the elucidations of specialists and by knowing more or less well what is objectively taking place in his body, it remains all the same hermetically sealed within itself and denies everyone entrance: the translation from objective language into the language of the subject can never fully succeed. This person's death, as soon as it first moves into visual range, becomes an unbearable personal vexation. He can only "repress" it or shove it off into regions where people think in emotionally empty concepts, but he can never really accept it: to assimilate death into the ego with the entire mass of its powerful specific gravity means to refuse life. People beat around the bush about death. Better: they express themselves by beating around the bush about it, testing it constantly with evasions, never venturing to make an approach mediated by speech as we are trying to do here. When someone has died, it is still possible to hear the closest family members tediously saying that he has "his peace" and that now, after so much toil, "he is well." In saying that, everyone knows that a cadaver cannot feel any kind of wellness, and that the chemical processes are already setting in that will lead to its total decomposition. And once you have expressed these conventional words in the death chamber, you may soon realize on the stairs that you were only thoughtlessly saying something that language and convention have offered you since time immemorial. Maybe you have misgivings that break up the grid of senseless talk and you murmur to yourself, "That one upstairs is neither well nor sick—how unimaginative! And what will happen with me? I already feel pressure here and there. I'm not going to get any better, good God!" But then you aren't calling on this God seriously either, if you consider yourself a believer and observe religious regulations. A natural-unnatural death is greater than God. Everyone has seen dead people before, but God remains constantly in hiding. That's the trick He lives by.

At this point we need to bear in mind that we are all mortal. Regardless of whether we have already heard the whir of the scythe over our head or not, we know about death. Psychologists think that such knowledge commences around the sixth or seventh year of life after the subject has succinctly posited itself as an ego. This knowledge becomes more intense each year, getting its own "feet," as it were. Humans live, therefore, beyond the evasions they organize for their self-defense, in a steadily crystallizing knowledge of death. They are like the man who builds a house knowing that it will be demolished at the roofing ceremony. He hopes for a "natural" death, stops brooding about himself with such a hope, turns the part of his ego that he abandoned and that dozes on in a vegetative state into an objective fact, and speaks an everyday language that has joined with a logical and precise one—or at least partly overlaps it. In doing this, he has a miserable intellectual and moral conscience, because the vegetative and numb ego that he thinks he's abandoned with his talk is actually his *real* ego: once death is postulated, this will not grant him a moment's peace ever again. He builds his house by the sweat of his brow, lays brick upon brick, fits in door and window frames—but it will all be in vain. Death takes on the features of unnaturalness and anti-nature. Unnaturalness? One must proceed with the greatest caution. Everyone, no matter what educational level he or she may be at, has both an uncertain and peremptory notion of nature. People know about the universe with a certain amount of exactitude; they have at least heard that the earth turns around the sun and at the same time around its own axis. A trace of geology is imparted to them in elementary school, by which their teachers have also given them a little bit of knowledge about gravity or electricity. When they advance a few levels higher in their young years, they get notions of physiology. Cells. Chemical processes. Haeckel's[4] notion, according to which the cells are autonomous citizens, billions of whom constitute our body and therefore form the "republic of cells," may be presented to them in one form or another. All at once they have to bring death into the realm of their knowledge, too; death, of which each has already heard beforehand, when Grandmother "went to God," Aunt Anna was stricken with a mortal heart attack, and the old neighbor, whose comic toddling may have been imitated for the amusement of friends, died of Parkinson's disease. Now, thanks to a more illuminating education in school, everyone knows that death is only the end, the natural end, of a development already set in motion at the beginning of life: the dying of the cells outstrips their ability to regenerate. —In the next hour of instruction we will concern ourselves further with the building up and dying off of the cells. Maybe some fitting words about the falling of the leaves in autumn as well. References in any case to the divine order that brings growth and decay into balance. Nothing disappears, of course. Mass and energy, capable of transformation into each other, survive for the world as a whole.

But there was something uncanny about the very idea of Grandmother's trip home to the Lord. Yesterday she was still lying in bed. It's true, she started wheezing rather heavily, but she still demanded water and was *thus there*. They took her corpse away, the pastor recommended her soul to God, and wished urgently with a murmur that the Prince of Darkness would not get that soul into his undoubtedly bloody hands. And now her place at the table and in her bed is empty. By the way, she died, as parents say, a natural death, fortunately when one considers how Uncle Adolf, who was always so jovial, lost his life in an Alpine accident, not to mention the woman from the next street, Frau Glücksmann, whom they gassed. Psst. Not a word more. Everyone gets one's turn someday, one way or another. In a few weeks Grandmother will be forgotten, just as jolly Uncle Adolf has been forgotten in the year that has passed.

The naturalness of death is drummed into us by reality in two ways. Once through the knowledge of events elucidated in school at every level; then through the people who in the end, after pouring forth a few tears, don't make too much of a fuss and talk more about someone's legacy than about someone's departure from the world; and finally by time that makes the dead and death forgotten. But it's all subject to recall. The talk of "going home," "dying," "death," "mortal danger," "mortal illness," and so on, is constantly renewed, so that for growing children there is no peace and they have to ask themselves, "Will I die, too, someday?" Naturally, one thinks, "In a natural way, perhaps at 50 years, but then I'll be ancient and until then there is still so much time, I'll never get there. Ah, if only I were already 19 instead of 15; then Maria the blonde, who always laughs so loud and crosses her legs in such a provocative way, would look at me instead of looking through me as if I were air." —Death is distant. It comes nearer. Its naturalness becomes more questionable. At the university the logic professor, whose lecture halls are always filled to the brim because he knows how to present his subject in a droll manner, says, "The so-called laws of nature are based on induction and faith in this is blind. You can all be immortal, my friends, it's not impossible to think so, any more than it is to think that tomorrow cold can come from fire." Laughter. Horror. It will certainly not get colder when I heat my room tomorrow and all of us, including me, will die. Nature has nothing to do with logic. Death is natural and I am already building the house that will collapse at the roofing ceremony. My death is beyond logic and habitual thought, for me it is *contrary to nature* in the highest degree, it is offensive to reason and to life. One cannot bear to think about it. —And where do you go in the evening, Gisèle? Would you like me to come with you?

The evening with Gisèle was nice. Only a few days later it became known that one of the city's well-known grain dealers had shot himself. His wife had left him, he was neglecting his business, getting into debt, running up bills he could not cover, and he was threatened with being taken into custody by the authorities. Since the collapse of the Reich, he had been saving the revolver he'd had as a noncommissioned officer, possibly to use someday on himself. Now he had taken it and shot himself in the temple in front of the mirror. At one time or another, sooner or later, everyone is confronted with what people call in German self-murder, and this confrontation occurs with such proximity to each of us that the act clearly has nothing to do with a chance newspaper report in small print. Suicide enters every human life at a definite point in time as gossip. With its appearance, an inquiry into the naturalness of death takes on a completely new, previously unknown dimension. That is to say, if death has never been fully acknowledged subjectively as a "natural" event related to one's own person, then suicide will appear at first to be downright uncanny. The house built by the grain merchant was not torn down when it was finished, he himself destroyed it deliberately—even willfully and with spirit, with high spirits and a strong will. "He's always been that way," the people say. "No wonder! And how can one do that to oneself! An uncovered bill of exchange, that's the ultimate. An adventurer. A man without vitality. A ruined man." The gossip is soon recognized as such and censured. At the same time that one becomes acquainted with voluntary death (not the knowledge of it, that should be clear; one never gets that far and, to the degree that one approaches it at all, one does so only in one's later years), one learns something about *échec*.

Let me explain why I am using a French word here. *Échec* means something like failure, defeat. But none of the German equivalents has the same phonetic expressive value (and thereby remarkably semantic value as well). *L'échec* with its dry sound (*son ton sec*), with its chopped-off, shattering noise, is a better word for rendering the sense of the irreversibility of total ruin. *L'échec* is a fateful word: thus it is used here in place of its clumsy ostensible equivalencies in German, that only sound heavy-handed, of which none are sufficient. The businessman who shot himself met with an *échec*. That means the world rejected him before death took him out of the world and rejected the world.

Basically, one can live in *échec*. But only in a disgraceful, almost "unnatural" way. For that reason the businessman thought that the only possible objection to his *échec* was voluntary death, an action to which people, with lowered voices as if dealing with some kind of abomination, give the name of "self-murder". Now *échec* stands as a threat in the background of everyone's existence, more conspicuously than death. One has to prove oneself. Will one be able to? Apprenticed mechanics have to maintain themselves as much as top managers do, as much as Communist Party functionaries do. There are always others who are still weaker. There are always others who are still stronger. The threat of *échec* is perhaps most clearly noticeable in a situation in life that I call the *"Abitur*-situation."[5] Oral examination. There is no way of avoiding it in one case, no mercy in another. Please translate. Interpret this line by Hölderlin. Solve the equation. Whoever can, can. Whoever can't, fails— and falls into a bottomless pit. Those who have it behind them, laugh easily. They laugh like fools. *Abiturients* hang above an abyss; the rope to which they are fastened proves again and again to be fragile. Those who fail—look at the way they come out. Parents and fellow students are the least of their concerns. They are full of understanding, after all people are enlightened. The *échec* is something that only the affected person experiences in its full inexorability. So he takes a pistol, like Heinrich Lindner in Emil Strauss's *Freund Hein* (Our friend Hein), a novel about a student that is still worth reading today. All at once the voluntary death of the grain merchant, who in the end was nothing more than an *Abiturient* who didn't pass, acquires that illuminating naturalness that Grandmother's death lacked. Wherever *échec* threatens constantly, in the form of failure in the *Abitur*, or bankruptcy, or a diatribe by a leading critic,[6] or the crippling decline of one's creative powers, or sickness, or the love that gives no tender response, or the trembling anxiety before an assault that the commanding officer disdainfully censures—here voluntary death becomes for everyone everywhere a promise full of potential. For reflective persons at the end of their chain of thought a natural death becomes the most extreme *échec*. You have lived and it was for nothing, because one day the world that you've been carrying inside you, the *entire* world, will perish. Forever vanished the nocturnal park at the spa where you received your first tongue-stroking kiss; gone the radiant premiere at which you finally stepped in front of the curtain alone, surrounded by applause; slipped away never to be seen again the tool with which the diamond was polished, the sewing awl with which you double-stitched soles for the delight of all those who still knew how to value proper handicraft. *Un instant, Monsieur le bourreau. Mais déjà le couperet tombe. L'échec ultime.* (One moment, Mister Executioner. But already the blade is falling. The ultimate *échec*.) Isn't it better to beat the blade that guillotines us all to the punch? To escape that *échec*, and the last one of all to boot, with a no that brings all rejoinders to silence?

Two concepts must be introduced here, which in the first section were already mentioned but since then could not be duly treated: *humanity and dignity. Voluntary death is a privilege of the human.* In his monumental work of 1975, *Les Suicides*, a book that from my point of view contains the last word of every suicidology so far published, Jean Baechler writes, "Suicide is specifically and universally human. . . . At the risk of upsetting animal lovers, I am saying that it seems certain that *animals* do not kill themselves. We all know stories about the dog who lay down to die on his master's grave or the cat who could not bear to outlive his mistress. These are touching stories, but unfortunately, when verification is possible, they appear to have been made up and produced by the imagination. . . . Children do not commit suicide any more than animals. . . . Below seven years of age, I have found no cases at all. . . . Among *genuine psychiatric* suicides, one does not encounter a subject where the annihilation of consciousness has progressed to the point of eclipsing his human character."[7] —A testimony to the humanity of those who desire a voluntary death, from a place that deserves every conceivable confidence!

Now to the second concept, which will concern us even more often. It is called "worth" or "dignity." Dignity can be established by a particular society, like Lt. Gustl's officer's dignity that forbade him to continue living after he had failed to live up to the code of honor demanded by his social standing as a royal and imperial officer. Dignity can be that of the merchant who held his social standing high enough to believe that without it he had no reputation after he went bankrupt and therefore preferred death to an existence without honor. It can be the dignity of Thomas Mann's Mijnheer Peeperkorn,[8] a virile dignity so annihilated by sexual impotence that only death—with vexation, of course, as we have already shown—can extinguish the disgrace. Jean Baechler himself, a man of facts and numbers, of methodological order, for whom all higher things, as it were, are distant and who never presumes to make any value judgments about life and death, writes in the scant two pages (of the 650 of the entire work) dedicated to the *philosophie du suicide* that voluntary death is an essential aspect of the *condition humaine*. "That suicide," he says, "confirms freedom, dignity, and the right to happiness seems to me to emerge clearly from the facts." Therefore, the humanity and dignity of each person—we're not talking about freedom here, we'll come to that later—are opposed to *échec*. They cannot bear it. Half smashed to pieces after the fall into *échec*, human beings lift themselves up in the name of their humanity and snatch death to themselves.

This is not a psychological concern and for that reason even the psychology of *échec* in particular is not up for discussion. There are two authorities that define the conditions under which a person's vital situation can be designated as *échec*: the subject and society. The judgments of both diverge, especially in the case of suicide. In most cases society rejects suicide, first of all for reasons connected to the preservation of the species, but in our civilization also under prior religious and ethical premises. In carrying out this rejection, psychologists and psychiatrists are society's faithful servants. The grain merchant killed himself? What a senseless act! After serving his sentence in jail and most likely after psychological and hygienic advice from an appointed expert, he could have lived on as a minor employee, and in the end he could even have been successful again. In any case, his unreason could have been steered to make him become what we all are: a useful member of society. In opposition to that, the subject sticks to its rights. It doesn't want to install itself comfortably in *échec*. It doesn't care about society, frequently not even about next of kin who are made unhappy by its choice to die—to a certain degree, for no one likes to live with the dead. It reaffirms one last time its dignity—and after it the deluge.

The waters do not encompass the earth, we don't need

a Noah's ark when someone says farewell to life of his own free will. Society, including the family, is insulted. In the end, it forgives a little—and forgets. The *échec* was not its affair but belonged to a subject disturbed for a moment or even one that had planned it for a long time. Unfortunately, as many before him had done already and certainly countless others will after him, the man died an unnatural death. What the community of the living doesn't know and cannot know, insofar as it presupposes that its continued existence is necessary, is of course the fact that the voluntary death was indeed hard for the suicide, like every death, but it was at the same time and to a high degree natural as well, even in its own applied sense. But then does the thought of the naturalness of voluntary death occur exclusively to suicides or suicidal persons? By no means. Those who always encounter the idea of death will say to themselves, as Max Frisch attests, at least playfully and at least once in their lives: "Since I am still only living in order to die, only building the house so that it will collapse at the roofing ceremony, it is better to flee from death into death," or—if they think further and more exactly—from the absurdity of existence into the absurdity of nothing.

To a large extent this concerns the degree to which they have an aversion to what has loftily been referred to as a "stimulating proliferation of being,"[9] that is, life. I am not holding my little finger out to psychology; I don't want it to take my whole hand; I am just commending myself with a little bow. If I dare to use the phrase *disgust with life*, it is not supposed to have any meaning for psychologists. From the standpoint of social-philosophical understanding, it is not socially acceptable for a human being to hate being flesh, to hate being able to touch himself, and it is also unacceptable to have to see what he doesn't wish to see, streets and faces and landscapes, just the usual sights. Neither socially acceptable nor accessible to psychology because the latter is still subordinate to a community that supports life, and anyone who is disgusted does not wish to know anything about the glories of creation. Take nourishment and eliminate excrement. Murder, shiver with pleasure, be murdered, trembling with fear. Be. And why is there anything at all instead of nothing? A false question par excellence; one has to meet it with a cool head and give logic its due. One nevertheless has to accept it, if one wants to do more than perspicaciously play mental games, and hopelessly try to answer. Disgusted with being (the stimulating proliferation of nothing, says our lofty authority) and life (a malignant tumor of being) we carefully consider the false question even as we are disgusted. *La nausée*, one of the basic constituents of a human being. It is no more possible to ignore it than eros, with the distinction that the latter is recognized by society because it is consistent with the logic of life, while the former, *la nausée*, is denied by civilization's howling rabble set on preserving the species.

By the way, I'm not taking a position. Not yet. What I am driving at is simply this: that prior to the consciousness of the *échec* that leads to voluntary death, as *échec in* life (failure of the *Abiturient*) and *échec of* life (certainty that the house will be torn down), there must be the feeling of disgust. To be normal is to overcome *échec*, and society applauds the brave man who doesn't let himself be frightened. The suicide is frightened. To someone who has constantly felt disgust with more or less intensity, the *échec in* life and *of* life becomes the totally horrible thing he is resolved to reject, in pride and mourning. He throws himself on the side of that tiny minority who do not want to participate any longer and who are called cowardly by every simpleton, as if there could be some kind of higher courage than the kind that defies the origin of every fear, the fear of death. The bravery of the potential suicide is certainly not arrogance. There always dwells within it an additional trace of shame that, derived from the logic of life, makes the person standing before the leap ask why it is specifically he or she that can't stand it, can't stick it out, when the others still . . .

It always happens that voluntary death is only for a moment more natural to suicides and the suicidal than a socially accepted natural death. They are still *living* while they are thinking and are thus with a part of their person paying tribute to the logic of life right up to their last breath, up to those final moments when they are without consciousness and only their body acts and reacts according to the logic of life, writhes and becomes distended; refusing to concede that the spirit of disgust, which is perhaps the very spirit itself, might win the upper hand—which upper hand, of course, loses everything and hangs slackly over the edge of the bed before rigor mortis gives it henceforth a senseless stability, senseless because it is promised to disintegration. Suicides are frightened, I am saying, frightened of the nothingness that they want to take to themselves but that won't embrace them, frightened also of the society that damns them (they are a part of a minority and thus virtually colonial slaves of life), the society that they know will set everything in motion to save them—or, to express it in modern terms, that will put them in its pocket again. Why do we make what is already hard enough for them even harder? Their no to being is surely absurd nonsense, but something they have to cope with in dignity.

Here I am going to call on the suicidologist Jean Baechler one last time, a man, I repeat, of the logic of life and anything but an existential pessimist. "The condition of good manners," he says, "is what affects the suicide, far from granting him any suitable value. Voluntary death remains rejected as a disgrace, even the suicide's immediate surroundings and associates are almost always looked at askance by his neighbors. The institutional positions of the church and the state have changed, they have dispensed with the external indications of disgrace. But public opinion has not yet gone so far and within it the old interdict, stemming no doubt from the Christian tradition, is alive."

Stemming from the latter, too, but *not only* from it. I knew a married couple whose son, a young lawyer for political delinquents, died a violent death in an African state; whether it was a case of suicide or murder could never be clarified. The father and the mother, however, were united in their loudly proclaimed opinion that they hoped that their son had been murdered and had not died by his own hand. The couple was religiously Jewish, anchored in Jewish tradition. To them murder seemed more natural than voluntary death, which in the world of their imagination was an ignominy. It is important to note that these two were harmless and thoroughly good-natured people. And yet self-murder, as they called the possible voluntary death of their son, was still something offensive that one did not even want to take into consideration, regardless even of the fact that a murder, executed by Africans who were adept at torture and mutilation, would have been something decisively more horrible. As far as I know there is not any expressed prohibition of suicide in the Old Testament. So the unhappy couple had not drawn such a highly astonishing position from following a religious tradition as much as from reasons lying beyond all custom and all religion. The father and mother did not want to acknowledge that their son could have broken with the logic of life, they did not want to recognize that first of all a natural death is not so natural, that second their son had chosen a voluntary death as the natural one for him.

If the most recent results of research in suicidology are accurate—about which I am certainly not entitled to make a judgment because I only know a comparably tiny section of the thousands of publications about suicide—then voluntary death occurs in all societies known to us, occurs at all times in every religious community. Of course, it was always carried out—at all times in various ways that can be studied, have already been studied to some degree, and are substantiated—only by an inconsiderable minority. "Why should I play the Roman fool, and die / On mine own sword?" asks Macbeth. The socially justified suicides—in China after the death of the master Confucius, in Greek antiquity when the philosopher Hegesias exhorted everyone to voluntary death, in the late Roman epoch when it was occasionally a matter of *bienséance* (decorum), among the Visigoths where the old threw themselves from cliffs in order to earn admission to paradise as a reward for their bravery—have only slight significance when viewed from the perspective of history. The logic of life triumphed and continues to triumph. Rightly so. On its side stand not only our instincts but, as I was able to explain in the first part, the logical principle itself because it is still not possible for reason—reason of being and of life—to weigh a not against something else, but only a something in comparison to another something. The equation $a = a$ is an expression of the primary experience of being and existence. The equation $nihil = nihil$ is senseless and against reason. Except that a small point must be considered: voluntary death *exists*. It exists, as we have been trying to show, as an answer to *échec*, as an objection against life, which hides within itself its own *échec* and is its own denial. Life is therefore both an affirmation and a negation and is thereby *absurd*, no less absurd than voluntary death, which only thus can be designated as "twice absurd," even must be so designated, because one who carries it out to the end remains enclosed with a part of one's person in the logic of life that one denies because one will indeed finally negate oneself. One breaks out and lies nonetheless in chains. One does not want to wait for the natural death that is recognized as against nature, yet which, as the natural itself, dressed in the fool's clothes of life, is an inexpressibly sweet enticement.

Heinrich Lindner, in *Freund Hein*, having flunked his *Abitur*, wanders with his pistol through the woods after the humiliating *Abitur*-celebration, determined on a voluntary death. Rays of sunlight fall through the leaves. Dew lies on the meadows. A brook babbles briskly, as the law of life commands. The 18-year-old allows himself first a few more steps, then a little rest, and says, pulling himself together, "The spirit is willing." But his flesh is weak and plots against him with the most amiable masks. He resists the lure, more a lure to be than a mere demand of the flesh to endure. Not only the strength of his spirit but also his disgust, rising up within him for a long time, lets him carry out the act he has commanded himself to do. And now not is equal to not: the absurd equation that we all write down while living whenever the shadow of death falls upon us "for no reason at all," is now worked out—for no reason at all. Or should I say that the principle of nothing was stronger than the principle of hope—which I've never believed in, despite all the historical and political sympathy I hold for Ernst Bloch, whose cheerful intellect conceived it? It would be premature to take up this question at this point. For the time being, we are only concerned with rehabilitating voluntary death as an act as natural or as unnatural as every other kind of death. Above all socially, because death, voluntary or not, cannot be defended philosophically. I am only trying to ensure that those who try to commit suicide and those who succeed, in spite of their situation as a minority, have the rights that every minority claims for itself. Fortunately, we have already come far enough in every progressive society so that the erotic minority is considered neither criminal nor sick. Homosexuals, men and women, are not put in quarantine until they are "cured." I don't see why the suicidal should remain the last great outsiders. Naturally their act vis-à-vis society is more negative than homoerotic behavior: the latter only rejects the logic of procreation, not that of existence. Still, it is a bad disposition for the human temperament contemptuously to disown the suicidals whose plans succeed and to treat as lunatics those whose don't.

In a small central European country that fancies itself to be especially progressive, every "rescued" attempted suicide who has not figured out how to conceal the act, is ex officio turned over to a psychiatric clinic. I will never forget the horrible and humiliating impression made on me by a young woman who had only spoken of her *intentions* to take her own life and who now, done up in a kind of penitential hair shirt, was sitting among lunatics, expecting the judgment of a couple of university-educated fools, compared to whom she had a vastly superior intellect. A commission of utter strangers had to decide whether and when she would be let free. What unbelievable impudence in a society that can only beat around the bush about death! Here redress is to be taken, but it can't be realized without breaking the arrogance of a science that knows nothing because it won't know anything of death. I have no illusions.

My little digression into an area that is not mine will certainly be the last one to bring any insight to the gentlemen who decide what makes sense and nonsense, who rob "self-murderers" of their freedom. As long as those who have nothing to do with psychology and psychiatry fail to pursue the goal that urgently promotes the conclusive recognition of the freedom to choose a voluntary death as an inalienable human right, things will remain as they are. Society will continue to "excommunicate" suicides and attempted suicides under the malicious pretext that through the act they've carried out or planned they have given up all claim to communion with others. For the kind of relief work I have in mind, anti-psychiatrists, authors like Michel Foucault or Deleuze and Guattari are needed, but they are not sufficient. One would also have to take great care that they do not ultimately cause more mischief, because their basic conception of mental suffering as a sickness of the social body shoots way over the mark. There is in fact a dementia that, in its rejection of the totality of experience, is not socially conditioned and therefore not socially curable: Anyone who steadfastly insists that he is the German King Henry IV, like the protagonist of Pirandello's play, is going out of his mind and is crazy. It is not possible to erect a society that could let him be right to the extent that it could make him into this historical personality. On the contrary, the society will have to ensure that he does not hire murderers to beat to death someone he thinks is Pope Gregory VII so that the way to Canossa is avenged.[10]

I have gotten off the subject, but not so far that I can't take up the thread again. Dementia and society could only enter into this discussion because society clearly considers potential suicides *grosso modo* to be fools or half demented, because it isn't able to enter into their closed world. But that's just what is being tried here—as far as is possible with the medium of language. We are speaking of two phenomena: *échec* and disgust with the world, the latter including within itself the disgust of death. Both are phenomena that have been robbed of their dignity by the sciences of psychology and psychiatry. They make them out to be sicknesses, knowing full well and consenting to the fact that sickness is a disgrace. (Who hasn't known a man who suffers a small stroke, but takes care of himself and stubbornly hides it no matter how well or badly off he is?) Branches of research think they know a good deal about what are, for them, the sickly conditions of disgust with the world and *échec*. In truth, they only know kinds of behavior. They don't know anything more about human beings than Konrad Lorenz understands about his beloved greylag geese.

Let's take a man who is melancholic. His mask is rigid, without expression, painful. The "patient" (for he had better be patient, given the laughable self-importance that is staged around him) withdraws from the world. Only seldom does science take a small step beyond behavioristic verification or free itself from previously given hypothetical speculations. Then one reads sentences like this one: "The past was disgraceful, the present is painful, the future nonexistent" (L. Colonna in the publication *Suicide et nosographie psychiatrique*). At one time or another this patient, having grown to be someone who was impatient, tried suicide. Was his past really disgraceful to him? In his sense definitely: in the feeling of *échec* he is summing up all the failures of his existence, which clearly amount to a stifling outcome. On the other hand, however, all the humiliations that he has suffered, all the troubles that were inflicted upon him, his disappointed hopes, all were still very much a part of him. He can only separate himself from them with difficulty. Freud's "pain of separation" is a cause of grief to him when he runs away from a future that he can only anticipate as new suffering, right into the hidden nonexistence of death, which by this time is for him the only natural way out: he has neither the time nor the desire to wait for a kind of dying that comes as something "natural" and against which, he knows, his agonizing body will writhe and swell insanely and without hope. How sick is this melancholic? How sick are the depressed? I do not have the right profession nor the qualifications to talk about these things in a discourse that would be accepted, even listened to, by scientific authority. It only seems to me, after all that I have read and have experienced myself, that the boundaries between psychic (and, by the way, physical) health and the realm of sickness are constantly drawn arbitrarily and according to whatever is in effect in society as the prevailing frame of reference. How sick were the visionaries, the mystics, the ecstatics? How healthy those whom Schopenhauer called the many-too-many, who in their appeal to common sense spoke nothing but the most outrageous nonsense? Only yesterday I read about a French minister of King Louis Philippe who said it was perfectly healthy for the 8-year-old children of workers to toil in workshops ten to twelve hours a day, otherwise they would just fool around in their leisure time. To us, the man was either a cad or mentally ill: to his fellow citizens and contemporaries he appeared to be an undoubtedly reasonable man, even a humane one. Didn't he think of the health of the children? I ask myself how sick I must be because I cannot refrain from the enjoyment of tobacco, long ago forbidden me by my physician. How sick am I when, in the midst of life, I try to have myself embraced by death and to justify the absurd logic of death on the same par as the no less absurd logic of life? If I perceive correctly, mental illness begins right at the point when someone sets misjudgments above the totality of experience, when someone maintains that he is what he is not, has been where he never was, has already died when he is in fact still alive. Depressed individuals or melancholics for whom "the past is disgraceful, the present painful, the future non-existent," are no more sick than homoerotic individuals. They are only *different*. Science thinks they've lost all sense of proportion; through a psychic "blowup" they've stirred up an insignificant unforeseen event, they've made an anthill into a mountain. The logical nonsense of such statements is obvious. The "thing" (the anthill in our case, or else the mountain) is never anything other than an intentional construction. A table is for me then and only then a table when I use it as such by working on it, by having my food served on it. It is no longer a table in the colloquial sense if I am always using it only as a ladder to help me paint the wall of my room. And it is altogether possible that I can get into de facto situations in which the anthill becomes a mountain to me, such as when I lie flat on the ground and squint to observe the creatures trotting up and down in a hurry. The "proportions" are measured by society. But in addition everyone still has his or her own measure at hand. My judgment, insofar as it does not call into question the totality of all experience, finally has to be recognized as the valid one. I am in a position to say: "The incident that seems inconsequential to all of you may certainly be such to you, that I don't deny; but for me it is a decisive event in life, decisive enough that on its account I'll give myself death."

Natural death: natural to me not only because I cannot intellectually assimilate the kind of death designated as natural by everyday language, but also because I am not willing to subject myself to a social judgment about what I am and what I do. To be sure, one's being and actions are essentially defined by *functionality*. Anyone who becomes a melancholic and pursues professional activity only with antipathy, thus insufficiently, and eventually not at all, who just cowers in bed to bide his or her time, is of no use to society and does not function. Therefore, society has to see to it that such a person gets "cured" by beating around the bush with psychotherapy, by electroshock, by chemical treatment, and if all that doesn't help, by exclusion and incarceration. Only when one finally gets into the fool's tower does one become invisible, stop disturbing people, and moreover get watched so well that it is not possible to choose to end one's life on one's own: thus the community of the busy has a good conscience. But I object and have to say that here social justice is not only committing a mistake that might still be pardonable, but an outrageous crime it must be vaguely conscious of. Psychotherapeutic talk that beats around the bush, electroshocks, and chemical preparations are ready to make someone who was *different* in one's own way into someone different in quite another way: an ego, imposed upon a human being, which ego is only the questionable product of external interventions that alienate one from one's own interests. Dentists and surgeons, it is true, also make external interventions, and no sensible human being would claim that an inflamed appendix should not be removed by an operation or an abscessed tooth not be extracted. But as far as the person of someone who is sick is concerned, entrails and teeth are the external world: anyone who has had an appendectomy has experienced nothing worse than someone who moves out of one apartment where he or she was disturbed by noise and into another. In this case it is the *res extensa* that is altered, for the good. But where depression and melancholy are concerned, where even a project to end one's own life is thwarted, there an injury occurs to the *res cogitans*, an injury that is worse than the most dreary psychic disposition can ever be. It doesn't mean a thing when the "cured," once they no longer know who they are and function as dimwits, say with gratitude that Dr. So-and-So prescribed for them a medicine and since then they see the world once again in a rosy light. In this case someone is babbling, having been denied any other speech.

So, at the worst, does everything finally boil down to the struggle between the ego and the others, the individual and society? Yes and no. In any case, the conflict is fought out or settled in favor of society, that's clear: it forms the repressive majority vis-à-vis the solitary ego. But those who have gone just far enough to repudiate the judgment of the majority, having looked in and seen how insurmountable the gap is between individuality and functionality on the one hand, between one's subjective condition and inter-subjective verification on the other, will certainly not be blindly hostile to this judgment (then they would be demented), but will quite probably limit it and refuse to recognize its binding force as universal and incontestable. They have detected in advance the perverse nature of a natural death: therefore they can no longer deprive suicides and potential suicides of their right to the naturalness of their freely chosen death. With that *the total image of the world is radically changed.* Death, which embraces us all at every hour, is no longer *le faux,* so designated by Sartre in a way that is logically difficult to attack but humanly insufficient. Even the face of death carries different features. Death cannot be repressed because it must not be repressed: a new humanism appears on the horizon, one that regards the principle of hope as justified, while at the same time recognizing the principle of nothing, in itself contradictory and yet inevitable. The suicide becomes a figure just as exemplary as the hero. Someone fleeing the world is not worse than someone who conquers the world—perhaps even a trace better. The majority may set up its law, one that changes and yet, in the meaning of its functionality, is eternally the same; but when the majority no longer has the last word, the word of a person with insight and comprehensive tolerance tips the scales.

Suicide is now hardly more of a scandal than poverty and sickness. It is no longer the crime of a dark and gloomy temperament (or, as they would have said in the Middle Ages, of a temperament possessed by demons), but an answer to the oppressive provocations of existence, especially the passage of time, in the stream of which we are swimming along and watching ourselves drown; bit by bit our ego starts to be washed away, when memories grow pale and when the reality of our person finally gets caught in a whirlpool that sweeps it into bottomless depths. What is suicide as natural death? A resounding no to the crushing, shattering *échec* of existence. The merchant killed himself? It was better than accepting his disgrace and waiting for society to forget his underhanded exchange practices. The *Abiturient* who flunked shot himself? He was not a misfit because of that; on the contrary he obviated the threat that he would become one. A melancholic drew the consequences from his dreary view of the world, of which no one may say that it was perverse. At the least we want to grant that he acted rationally, particularly that he acted according to his own, inalienable reason. "One has to live in the end," people say in their people's wisdom. One does not have to, especially because in any case everything boils down to the fact that on a particular day that will certainly come we not only do not have to live but *must* not live. There is a reaper;

his name is Death.[11] Everyone can take the scythe in hand and swing it for oneself. The limits of the metaphor have already been reached. One cannot mow oneself down. But not to have to live: this becomes a commandment wherever dignity and liberty forbid abominable conditions to the anti-nature of a living toward death, of a life in *échec*. The subject decides for itself in its full sovereignty. That doesn't mean "against society." The individual can destroy what he or she owns, which never really was one's own, for the sake of an authenticity about which one is anxious. One lays hands on oneself.—Of this we hear in what follows.

III. To Lay Hands on Oneself

Yet another phrase, drawn from the language of reality, then taken further from it, finally neglected again, so that today it has an almost archaic character: *to lay hands on oneself.*

I confess that it has always appeared so thoroughly penetrating, even pervasive, to me that I still feel inclined to use it, no matter how out of fashion it may sound. To lay hands on oneself. A frightful act of suicide occurs to me, one that Gabriel Deshaies speaks about in his *La psychologie du suicide*, a book that appeared in 1947 and, as far as I know, has not been translated.

A blacksmith placed his head between the blocks of a vise and with his right hand turned the apparatus until his skull broke to pieces. Other ways of death—*Ways of Death*, wasn't that to be the title of the last book by Ingeborg Bachmann?[1]—likewise cruel, are no doubt known to everyone. A man who cuts through his throat with a razor. The Japanese writer and warrior Mishima[2] thrusts the point of his saber into his belly, as the ritual commands. A convict tears his shirt to pieces, twists from it a cord, winds it around his neck, and hangs himself from the bars of his cell. Violent ways of death: one's hand is actually applied. To what? To a body that for the suicide is a part of his or her ego. The ego and the body: what about them? They are one and they are two: object of potential and actual suicides and subject, as such insurmountable, even if vulnerable and capable of annihilation. There is no doubt that someone who voluntarily wants to die must have a peculiar relationship to these two manifestations of unity and duality—perhaps a psychologist would call it a "narcissistic" relationship (which would not exclude auto-aggression; but we'll take up psychological hypotheses later, at the proper time).

Now we are standing before the naked fact that an ego and a body are destroyed—by the same ego, the same body. How do things stand with the latter? In comparison to the ego, as I was saying, the body is composed of bodily events, parts of the body, heart, stomach, kidneys, etc., and they are part of "the outside world." There is much to be added here, for in fact the outer and the inner, or else the within, are so constituted that they often permeate each other, then again flee from one another, and later are so foreign to one another that it seems that they had never known each other. The relationship of body and ego is perhaps the most mysterious complex of our lived existence or, if one prefers, of our subjectivity or our being-for-itself. We are not aware of our body during everyday existence. To our being-in-the-world our body is what Sartre called *le négligé, le passé sous silence*, neglected, one scarcely speaks of it, doesn't think of it. The body is enclosed in an ego that is, for its part, also outside, elsewhere, in the space of the world, where it annulls itself (*se néantise*) to realize its project. We *are* our body: we do not *have* it. It is, as I wrote when I introduced the subject, the other, it is external world, definitely. Just as definitely, however, we become conscious of it as a foreign body only when we see it with the eyes of the other (as for example when we inform ourselves through science about its functions) or when it becomes a *burden*. But even in this case, when for example we would like to "jump out of our skin," as the expression goes, because of pain, then the body is both hostile and our own: the skin we want to be rid of, the skin we want to shed, is still ours, a part of our ego. "*Le négligé*" is the body only when it conveys world to us. In the high jump it is air and flight; while skiing it becomes dusty snow and icy wind.

Can we say that in everyday life, unencumbered by the body, when we are running ahead, when our arm turns the car's gearshift into action, that we are alienated from our body? Maybe. But since an act of alienation presupposes a prior being-with-oneself, which is not the case in all conditions, it is better to speak of a state of not yet possessing our body. It carries us, a faithful servant who, like a dumb waiter, disappears on soft shoes when his service is finished and we fall into sleep. Our servant revolts when we are sick. Then we are seized with rage against him, or instead against the part that is painfully mortifying us. And we answer. The "damned toe" that hurts us becomes a personal adversary that we now revile, from whom we bristlingly demand that it "leave us in peace." At the same time, the toe is ours: we do not wish it to be amputated, we only want it once again to *passer sous silence*, not to be noticed. Even the tooth, which in its brittle materiality is more foreign to us in the neurological sense than the toe and which we, when its periodontal membrane is infected, have to have torn out by the dentist (people say, "I have to have the cursed tooth removed, it's tormenting me"), becomes in the moment of its extraction and for a while longer something that to our dismay belongs to us, that we melancholically miss, and whose nonexistence, to which the gap in our mouth is a witness, diminishes our ego. We are "less" after the extraction, we are ashamed of the gap, and from much deeper reasons than merely aesthetic ones. Why should the asymmetry that a missing tooth gives to our face not have something striking, something *à part*, about it? Apart, quite right: we are *à part* with it, different from the others, less than they. And, before the replacement is artificially constructed and fitted in, we avoid any kind of smile.—

But is it an issue of a tooth, of a toe, even of an arm, a leg? Unfortunately, it is not: when we are at the point of voluntary death, when we are laying hands on ourselves, it is an issue of the *entire body*, which was the gestalt and support of our ego, alien and our own, *le passé sous silence*, but about which henceforth we will not only not talk (for we will no longer exist), but which will no longer speak itself since there is no one who can hear its voice. It will become something in the hands of the physicians who conduct the autopsy, something for the pallbearers who ease it into the grave. So it happens that even prior to standing immediately before the leap, we are aware of our body with an intimacy we've never previously felt. A special role is played here by the *head*. I often stand on the balcony of a particular seventeenth floor, then climb over the railing (fortunately I am always free of dizziness) and, keeping only my left hand fastened to the iron bars of the railing, hold my body far out over the void and stare into the depths. I only need to let go. How will my body plummet down? In the elegant turns of a corkscrew, as do the springboard divers I so often admire ? Or like a stone? Headfirst, I fancy, and anticipate in my imagination how my skull shatters to pieces on the asphalt. Or drowning, somewhere on the coast of the North Sea. Water at the legs, water that rises slowly, to the breast, on above it, to the lips. The head will try to remain a while longer above the waves, bursting with gurgling flute music. Until it disappears, and then what the people pull up on the beach is a thing, *une chose*, not someone who has drowned, but a something that no longer has anything to do with a human being and an ego. The guillotine: *déjà le couperet tombe* (the blade is already falling). Cutting off the head is the most drastic performance of annihilation. I even have the head in mind when I think only very indirectly of laying hands on myself, as when I swallow those pills that really make sleep the twin brother of death. Will my head hang over the edge of the bed? Will my eyes be wide open? As always: with my head's definitive reification I also become a thing. And remember, none of this has anything to do with the knowledge that the head is the site of my cortex, but I am speaking of a basic element in the experience of the ego. It is not a coincidence that blows to the head are considered the most ignominious of all humiliations that one can think of (it is well-known that one should never hit children in the face). We know about our head and its sovereign nature long before we possess the least physiological knowledge. Is *it* therefore our ego? Not the entire ego, that is obvious, but the part which, ranked highest, is first experienced

phenomenally. Those who step to the threshold of voluntary death carry on the great dialogue with their body, their
head, and their ego as they never have before. There are
many stages, countless conversational nuances, changing
aspects—many more than I can do justice to here.

So let's take a little from this fullness. The stirring of
tenderness for something about to be abolished, soon followed by decomposition, where an ego no longer existing
and a body that has become mere stuff will be fully united
in their nothingness—for no reason at all. "Pain of separation," as Freud puts it, before the farewell from what is both
most alien and most one's own, the body. Hand that now
touches the other hand so that touching and touched are
no longer to be kept apart: it will disintegrate—"This hand
is falling," as it says in the poem.[3] It still feels itself and feels
the other. The hands stroke one another, loving ones who
stand at a provincial railroad station and in the brazen din
tell each other, it's over and never again—but are still with
each other. Arms, legs, sex, how will they look in the phases
of dissolution? They are still there, alien and primitively one's
own, despised, even rejected, but still loved. Neck that the
cord will throttle: it has to be treated well before it no longer
is a part of my being-in-the-world, instead of just in the
world that is the world of others; neck that is the lasting
matter of the entire cosmos, to which that cosmos, which
does not know itself, is completely indifferent. The tenderness toward one's own body, already renounced because
the ego it carried is not permitted to exist any longer, is
distantly related to masturbation. Like the latter, it forms a
circulus. The lines that led outward, that encountered objects, other bodies, and came to their end, have all turned

around and end in one another in a senseless circle that corresponds to a senseless deed. "Only through human reality is there a world," says Sartre. But here the still-existing human reality is, in a masturbatory way, entirely dependent on itself, having relinquished the world to the extent that we have to ask: Is it still a human reality that is tenderly carrying on at this point with its own corporality? Even here the answer incessantly and monotonously moving through this discourse is valid: yes and no. It *is* a human reality since the body is certainly still feeling itself in the ego, regardless of whether it is in a frenzy (over cutting through the gullet) or in pain of separation if the choice is the gentle death of sleep made possible for us by the chemical industry. It is no longer human reality when another glance falls into the world according to which our consciousness should surely break open, but which will be thrown away in the next moment like a shabby piece of clothing. With that the world and the ego (which demanded the world as its due and took it up into itself just as, vice versa, the ego was received by the world) come to that end prescribed for each as law from the very beginning. The masturbation ends without orgasm. Suicides become tired of searching for their body. Their hands no longer stroke each other, the train that takes one lover from the other has already departed, a shrill whistle resounds. The one left behind is alone: an ego.

And the ego relentlessly constitutes itself right up to the last moment. Even when it no longer transcends itself as an intentional consciousness according to its own possibilities, it simply doesn't see such possibilities any longer and is still only by itself. But what does that mean? Most likely that the ego—already half out of the world, hostile to it, giving notice to its own project—is subsiding and again subsiding. I am; I shall not be, but I am. Am what? Am I. But who am I? I (and even now a whole world, of course without a future and passed away, but whose shadows still emerge in flight: a child in the park, blind and unruly in the haste of hide-and-seek; a kiss, allowed to the boy in a nocturnal park and given; departure from Yellowstone National Park, the "Roaring Mountain" in back; but everything already fully grown, made pale by time, which got it over and done with in a jiffy). Who am I? The body that also is already slipping away. Still more precisely: the face, which is body and perhaps more than that. It wants to see itself in the mirror when someone dies by his or her own hand (people who shoot themselves are often found in their blood in front of a mirror). If the face finds itself, it finds eyes that now strain to stare at each other in fours, a mouth distorted with fear. The face that meets itself does not yet have its ego. In that face, the ego does not yet have itself. Something like dread arises, something different from the suicide's fear that is stacked up inside. Whenever as a matter of course one says to oneself, "So that's what I am. But why am I that?" The ego's experience of horror in front of the mirror is not reserved for the suicidal. It also turns up as an everyday phenomenon and, by the way, can hardly ever be produced by a willful decision. As soon as it happens, it has the character of a sudden fall. The observing ego, banned from the image in the mirror, falls from crag to crag;[4] every one of them is another ego but provides no foothold, so that the depressing plunge only ends when the man, drawing a deep breath, but with the hunch that he has now become poorer and that through his ineptitude he has given up something precious, goes back to his working day. In any case, a suicidal constitution—disgust with the world, claustrophobia from the four walls closing in on each other as one hammers one's head against them—naturally brings potential suicides distressingly close to such shadowboxing. For it is certainly the case that the ego, no matter where it hides and what it is, a "bundle of feelings" or an immanent manifestation of the transcendental subject, is standing at the end of itself. It has denied the world and, along with that, its own self: it has to get rid of itself and partly feels itself as a has-been, already decomposing. At this point, the ego tries for the last time to reach itself. Four eyes stare, two mouths are twisted into cruel scorn or great pain. In such moments the ego, no longer body and hardly even being-in-the-world, definitely no longer striding-into-the-world, becomes frightened: for a moment it loves itself very much, coddles whatever it once was, and won't believe it has made its case so badly that it has to disappear in such a disreputable way. But at this point it is already losing itself, giving itself up, turning itself backward toward pure and simple phases that it has overcome, turning itself into a pale shadow-existence that no longer is. All consciousness, it is said, is *consciousness of something*. If the ego of the suicidal loses itself in its memories, it is still consciousness of precisely those. It was formerly pure consciousness of itself, in its downfall; it already contained something of masturbation and death.

Something of death; how harmless! For now death itself, as the most extreme form of irreversibility, confronts both suicidal and suicide—it is the end result, *exitus letalis* or rescue, here almost without significance—; now the question is about death as killing oneself and before which a human life, as an *Abiturient* of being or not being, has to stand the test. Nothing is to be taken away from what I just stated about the horror or dread of the ego's vain quest. The fright is great in any case, even when it is not a part of the preparations for suicide. But once suicide is set in motion, then the dread of emptiness, the *horror vacui* in the face of the riddle of the ego is likely to be hideously present, but still swallowed up by the naked fear of death, the entirely extrapersonal, desperate resistance of biological nature. Confronted with suicide we are always like the piglet whose squeals wrench our ears and hearts as it is dragged to slaughter. Gurgling water in which we drown. The way the left hand holds the skin to stretch out the throat while the right hand applies the razorblade. The head smashing on the asphalt. The strangling cord around the neck. The burning and detonation of the shot against the temple. All of which, however, once again, doesn't mean that there could not be present at the same time, when we lay hands on ourselves, when our ego loses itself in self-dissolution and—perhaps for the first time—totally realizes itself, a never previously known feeling of happiness. For now we are done with existing, with *ex-sistere*. No longer do we have to negate our constantly petrified being, the Sartrian *être*, while we step out of ourselves and, taking action, become world. For Sartre a state of being that doesn't know how to negate itself, and therefore permanently cancel itself in order to rise *ad infinitum* in the world, leads to disgust. But this disgust can also be understood in the opposite sense as an aversion to the effort to *ex-sistere*. More simply expressed: when the *Abiturient* finally says to himself, "Everything's turning out badly anyway but it won't concern me anymore, I don't care in the least about school and the life its drudgery is supposed to prepare one for," then a certain peace enters into his psyche. A peace, to be sure, in which fear is lurking: biological fear, fear of the most extreme pain of separation, fear of never again being afraid. But still again peace, the contradictory basic constitution of the human being, and the ambivalent not-only-but-also keep him company on the way to the death camp.

It is asked and I ask myself if, beyond the disgust with existence, there is a more general hypothesis to understand a person's disposition to choose death, voluntarily, even—I repeat—under the most unbearable forms of pressure. And here we find ourselves once again outside the realm of psychology, even though it must unavoidably force its way into our description of these matters, certainly phenomenal in nature, yet pertaining to the psyche as well—just as phenomenology, I am convinced, has its origin in the psychic constitutions of phenomenologists. Husserl, Sartre, Merleau-Ponty[5] were introspectively directed thinkers: what they brought to light was the knowledge of their own psychic constitution, clarified by having been conducted through channels of their reflection. Because psychology is once again intruding into this investigation, even though we don't want to stretch even our little finger out to it, let's accept that we can't avoid coming up against Freud when thinking about voluntary death, and even death in general. Later, as we progress, we will have to deal with psychological theories of suicide. Here, faced with the disposition toward voluntary death, with the question through which disgust with existence and aversion to the world might be explained, we are dealing with that disputed idea of Freud's which with few exceptions his descendants avoided: with the *death instinct*. "What follows now is speculation, often a long, drawn-out questioning speculation that each according to his particular outlook will appreciate or neglect," he says in *Beyond the Pleasure Principle*, the work whose hypothesis of the death instinct let loose in its time quite a bit of astonishment in the camp of psychoanalytic orthodoxy. Even if we want to avoid psychoanalysis here, too, the concept of "speculation" is very important to us, for "speculation," "often a long, drawn-out questioning" kind, as Freud confesses, is what we're doing here. And how could it ever be otherwise? The alternative would be nothing more than a strained effort to string along and classify data and facts, a new "psychological" interpretation that would have to be, as I've said, in comical disproportion to the event. So let's take up Freud's speculation and carry it forward: we'll see where we get with it.

It is widely known that for Freud the death instinct is that which opposes the life-preserving instincts. It amounts to an instinct of destruction, destruction of oneself and of others. "Our point of view," writes Freud in *Beyond the Pleasure Principle*, "was right from the beginning a dualistic one and today it is even more clearly so than previously since we no longer call the opposites ego- and sex-instincts, but life- and death-instincts." —Do I have to say that this sounds good to my ears, that this dualism completely corresponds— at least initially—to what I have called the primal contradiction of life; that to me the death instinct, which the newer psychoanalysis scarcely wants to pay attention to, appears useful as a generic concept to which my speculation about disgust with the *ex-sistere* could be subordinated? It seems to me that this hypothesis, a speculation of the 67-year-old Freud during the writing of *Beyond the Pleasure Principle*, has been neglected: after all, *voluntary death exists*, a conclusion that seems to provide evidence for the validity of Freud's hypothesis. Certainly, I have reservations. I have my doubts and even try to supplement the hypothesis at my own expense. Consequently, the compound "death instinct" has become even for me a difficult question. An instinct never operates in a void, but thrusts us into the tropically rampant fullness of being. It is *grosso modo* the Schopenhauerian "will," the will to live, the will to expand one's ego out into the world. The will, quite simply, to *be*. In the case of voluntary death, however, and of the disgust that precedes it, even perhaps conditions it, the state of being according to which the instinct drives us, is negated. It was Freud's pupil Edoardo Weiss who called his master's death instinct "Destrudo" with a felicitous latinate and abstract term. But even more destructive furor and aggression are clearly elements of life.

We, however, are dealing with death, whose pale nonentity sweeps even the final remains of the rubble away after the act of destruction. I am going to introduce a concept that, I think, accords better with the state of affairs, even if it contradicts every single psychological theory: an *inclination toward death*. Let's first take the phrase as a hieroglyphic. An inclination is an inclination toward something, a downward incline toward something, giving us a geotropism, a sign that points to the earth to which we belong. An inclination is also a dis-inclination, a disinclination with respect to life and being. It is a posture or more correctly the giving up of a posture and in that sense something passive. The inclination toward death is not so much formed as it is suffered, even when the suffering is a flight from the pain of life. It is concave, not convex. But in that case doesn't the empirical basis of such speculation have its most extreme point of reference in voluntary death, a highly active event? I cut my throat. I jump from the highest platform of the Eiffel Tower to the macadam of Paris. I put the cold bore of the revolver to my temple. I hoard sleeping tablets, write farewell letters, start my car in order to reach the place where, with a slight turning of the steering wheel, I can drive the vehicle as well as my person into a rocky abyss. I tie the rope, kick the stool away with my foot so that I come to hang in the emptiness and thus throttle my breathing passages. Like the blacksmith that Deshaies reports about, I even turn with my right hand the vise between whose blocks my skull is placed and begin to hear it cracking even before all is finished. Are not all of these outrageous, violent actions of laying hands on oneself irrefutable proofs in favor of a concept of an *instinct* and against my gentle idea of an *inclination*? I am just as uncertain as Freud probably once was when he was making his speculations public, quite to the displeasure of his adherents. And it would be ridiculous to deny the effort of will that voluntary death demands of us. I only know from my own experience and from my knowledge of the literature on the subject, and in spite of the fact that up to the last moment the life instinct is still in effect in our consciousness and elsewhere, that this effort of will is perhaps more modest than anyone may think who is not affected and does not gravitate toward voluntary death. Suicide is certainly much more than the pure act of getting rid of oneself. It is a long process of gravitating toward the earth, of approaching the earth, a summing up of many ciphers of humiliation that are not accepted by the dignity and humanity of the suicide, it is—and I am using once more an unfortunately untranslatable French word—*un chemine-ment*, a way of advancing along a road upon which, who knows, perhaps one's way is paved right from the beginning. If I'm not wrong, then the inclination toward death is an experience that everyone could make in oneself as long as one were determined to seek incessantly. It is contained in every kind of resignation, in every form of laziness, in every act of letting-oneself-go—for whoever lets oneself go is already voluntarily inclined toward that place everyone has at the end. Then wouldn't it be the case that suicide, against all that I have been boldly claiming, would not be *voluntary and free*? Would it be just a leaning toward an inborn inclination? Nothing but one's own acceptance of that ultimate absence of freedom that is nonbeing, and in whose fetters we allow ourselves to be beaten? Not quite. The inclination, I am saying, exists; but the life instinct also exists and whoever chooses voluntary death, elects something that, compared to the life instinct, is the weaker. One says, "To Hell with the strong!" as one gives in to the inclination toward death in opposition to the life-instinct. And if I was saying that one's way is paved to suicide right from the beginning, that cannot mean, nor does it intend to mean, that even a suicide would not succumb to the will to be and to live or would be conditioned by it. One of them eats in the evening before taking his hoarded pills. He gives the stupid biological driving force what it demands. But he gravitates toward the hotel room upstairs, where his farewell letters lie on the table along with the money for the hotel bill and his accumulated barbiturates, and he won't let himself be driven anymore. The earth will have him, but not in the way the poet meant it.[6] The thought of becoming dust is just as frightening as it is comforting. Is this charitable act of letting oneself die the expression of a desire, concluded by Freud to derive from the general compulsion of children and neurotics to repeat, "to return," to follow, as it literally states, "the urge dwelling within organic life to recover an earlier condition?" But which one? The anorganic, out of which we became an organism thanks to a "chance hit," as Jacques Monod says—the anorganic was not a "condition" we could relate to ourselves. Nonliving matter does not know and experience a way of being a condition. Our inclination toward death, insofar as we may apply this speculative concept, is therefore not a way back. Even less a way forward. It moves according to one's inability to situate the negating not.—With which we once more come up hard against the limits of language, which are an expression of the limits of being.

And there is such a fuss, so much effort is made to achieve dignity, so much human pride goes into an action that, because it is so indescribable, must also appear to be senseless! The principle of nothing is empty, no doubt about it, in comparison to the principle of hope, which encompasses all possibilities of life, the great, intensive, life experienced with reflection. But it is not only empty but also powerful, because it is the real finality of us all. This power, the power of emptiness, of what is beyond words, empty mightiness, which cannot be summarily described by any sign, is not attainable through any speculation, even though it may eventually be something we tentatively call, knowing well the insufficiency of the word, the "inclination toward death." I know that it is simpler merely to speak of a *taedium vitae* and to resolve this in whatever empirically determined conditions precede "self-murder", as they say. To be a match for the conflicts that the subject doesn't believe; "anomie"; the conditions according to Durkheim that lead to suicide, under which the action of an individual is out of order with respect to society: all of these psychological approximations are often contradictory among themselves, sometimes thoroughly assured empirically, constantly revisable and in need of revision, so much so that whoever reads a number of suicidological writings, outside of a few statistical facts, which, however are frequently disputed by others, knows in the end less about voluntary death than he or she knew before. Still, it is certainly necessary to form suicidological concepts again and again and to confront them with the totality of experience: psychology is a serious science to which we owe considerable insights, even if they are never definitive and always society's business, not the subject's.

It is therefore difficult to oppose anyone who speaks of *taedium vitae* rather than an inclination toward death. One cannot find any convincing arguments for the fact that voluntary death is an inclination toward a nowhere. But to speak from the place I come from, from a firsthand lived experience, to perceive the inclination to death as a *donnée immédiate de la conscience* (an immediate fact of consciousness), is to persist in a standpoint against the scientific method. I still know very well how it was when I awoke after what was later reported to me as a thirty-hour coma. Fettered, drilled through with tubes, fitted on both wrists with painful devices for my artificial nourishment. Delivered and surrendered to a couple of nurses who came and went, washed me, cleaned my bed, put thermometers in my mouth, and did everything quite matter-of-factly, as if I were already a thing, *une chose*. The earth did not have me yet: the world had me again and I had a world in which I was to project myself in order that I would once again be all world myself. I was full of a deep bitterness against all those who meant well who had done this disgrace to me. I became aggressive. I hated. And knew, I who had previously been intimately acquainted with death and its special form of voluntary death, I knew better than ever before that I was inclined to die and that the rescue, about which the physician boasted, belonged to the worst that had ever been done to me—and that was not a little. Enough. I will be no more convincing with my private experience than with my circular discussion of death. Besides, I'd rather be a witness than be convincing.

That said on behalf of everyone else rather than me. In a life that has already dragged on in its tired way for a long time, one has certainly heard and seen so much that one no longer needs the verifiable case histories that are so dear to scientific psychology: every individual case that makes one look up and fearfully hearken to the darkness stands for numerous others. Take Else G., 38 years old, exactly twice as old as the man who loved her and was loved in return without in the least being mothered; people thought of it as something ranging from the ridiculous to the repulsive. To the two of them it was as natural as death. She always carried a quantity of veronal tablets with her. She had had a prescription pad with the name of a nonexisting physician printed on it and wrote out her own prescriptions as needed.

She was said to have made several attempts at suicide and an air of mysterious rumor surrounded her person. People considered her to be high-strung and did not believe her theatrical plunges into sleep. In fact, most of the time the dose was so inadequate that even a lay person, which she no longer was, must have known that she had taken too little of the stuff. Voluntary death was a part of the way she led her life and she often spoke ironically about it herself. I never took her repeatedly new attempts seriously. Then we lost contact with one another and didn't see each other any more, until one day the news came that Else G. had poisoned herself: she was found dead in a hotel room in Amsterdam. Amsterdam, windy and foggy city of water and death, a backdrop well-chosen for dying, better than Venice. —One day I'll do it, this woman always said, with an uncertain sound to her voice and a thin, scoffing smile; now all at once it had the background of Amsterdam's reality.

Suicidologists say that it is a big mistake not to take seriously what a potential suicide says in jest. Voluntary death is a stubborn companion throughout life—a cavalier in black with the pale face of Hauff's man in the moon[7] (the suicidologists don't say that anymore, it wouldn't be serious). But since I'm not a serious person, like Else G. up to the moment when she increased the dose of her pills to three times as much as what she was used to, I talk without restraint of a deathly pale companion dressed in black: it is an allegory, an image with a meaning, an image of the inclination toward death that induces contemplation. I don't want to desist from it as a hypothesis, even if the number of successful suicides still only comes approximately to the slight amount of one in comparison to the majoritarian impact of the ten thousand who are mowed down by the reaper. And besides: the numbers don't say anything. First of all, a subsequently "rescued" potential suicide is often at the moment of the act a deadly earnest real suicide, so much so that the distinction between suicides and suicidals that I, following the suicidologists, thought was necessary to make my point, is quite arbitrary; and second, there are those accordingly designated "gray areas" in which embarrassed suicidals romp about, intimidated by the logic of life and a life-preserving society, acting as if they had never been suicidal.

Those who break through the self-protective aura preserving the species and give in to the inclination toward death, whether because an *échec* has brutally overwhelmed them and told them, "You are a nothing, now finally be *not*"; or because they have recognized the ultimate *échec* of every human existence and want to lay hands on themselves before hands—the hands of cancer, the hands of a heart attack, the hands of diabetes, etc.—are laid on them; those who thus give themselves up and deliver themselves over will always do so in a way conditioned by external circumstances. Ways of death. An officer concerned about his honor at the gambling table or in a foolish verbal exchange will reach for a firearm. It is his thing, he knows its mechanisms, he is familiar with its click just as he is with the body of his mistress. A man living near the coast of the North Sea will perhaps stride upright into the water, as once did Ludwig II of Bavaria, knowing that at flood-tide his ability to swim won't be able to match the power of the rising body of the sea. Physicians and pharmacists will take poison.

Anyone who lives on the seventeenth floor of a tall building must be tempted: the plunging depth, hardly noticed previously because one's glance goes far out across the countryside, now becomes a magnet for the leaning, tilting, and downward propensity toward one's senseless ownness. Even the blacksmith's horrifying way of death, pressing his skull between iron blocks, becomes understandable now: he has always worked with this tool, so let it be the tool of his final work. For all of them, those who hang themselves, shoot themselves, swallow poison, jump, go into the water, open their arteries, the *inclination toward death* is decisive, logically subordinate to their outraged disgust with life as well as their submissive *taedium vitae*.

Then there are those who are not recorded at all, who can't even hypothetically be placed in the gray zones: they let themselves die, without contradiction (as once did the "mussulmen" in the concentration camps who were much too weak to have had the strength to run to the electrified barbed wire), or who live in such a way as to accelerate their being-toward-death. "At the rate you're working you're certainly going to die," says the physician. "I'm warning you, it's time to take it easy." But that is out of the question; on the contrary, the reins choking the life out of the man are pulled even harder. And what was Sartre thinking when he was writing his *Critique of Dialectical Reason* and taking up to twenty-five corydran pills a day? Oh no, not of death, that would be too much of a contradiction of his doctrine. He was thinking of his work, with which he was striding into the world, gathering world, creating world. But maybe *something in him was thinking of death*, maybe he was tilting in that direction even as he thought he was quickening his pace. Who knows? Who knows of the many who, against the advice of their doctor, even against every simple, reasonable piece of advice of life itself, are living to snatch up their hours only to be snatched away more quickly? The businessman who shortens his nights and by day actually seeks stimuli he should avoid, then works himself to death "for the business," "for his family," as it is said. The writer who destroys the tool of his profession, his head, by whipping himself to work with alcohol and pep pills and destroys his heart by chain-smoking, practices utter nonsense "for his work," according to the logic of life—after his death a few colleagues respectfully say that he died on the field of a writer's honor, "for his work." It is clearly impossible to count all of them among the suicides. I wouldn't like to call them even suicidal. I just think that it doesn't really ring true to talk of this sacrifice "for his work," "for his family," just as it's probably inaccurate when we accept martyrs ("to freedom," "to faith," "to country," "to a good cause") as simply as history hands them down to us. I'd rather vote in favor of considering, even in obscure cases, the hypothesis of the inclination toward death and thinking of these martyrs as yielding to it even as they were being heroes for the world or were the famous "candles burning at both ends." An example occurs to me, which merely by mentioning will stimulate contradiction and even make me have to put up with the reproach of blasphemy: Christ's crucifixion. If we recognize the Rabbi Jeshua as an historical figure, which is disputable but by no means absurd, and if we further do *not* see the Son of God and the Savior in this militant prophet of love, then we will perhaps recognize his terrifying death as a *suicide en puissance* (potential suicide). We'll say in any case that he yielded to the inclination toward death, just as his head, inclined on the cross toward the earth, so movingly addresses us from every image of that scene; we will feel as if the crucified had previously not only cried out for his God without understanding that He was abandoning him, but also that he was telling humanity, "It's all right, for better or worse, pass on, it doesn't matter."

Of course, one thing makes a razor-sharp distinction between both the silent quasi-suicides who toil their way to death as well as the heroes and martyrs on the one hand and the authentic suicides and attempted suicides on the other: none of them are fully aware of the moment *before the leap* as a concrete experience, and that the voluntary nature of their death is always only partial. The chain-smoking writer is not sure that in the shortest period of time death will actually appear—and besides, the shortness of this period, even the assumption that one can grasp it within a given period of time ("It can't last longer than another year, six, three months") cannot be experienced in advance. Whatever happens, the hero does not have to be hit by an enemy bullet when he obviously runs into the arms of death in an attack against a tank. The martyr can be spared—and even the Rabbi Jeshua would basically have liked to have had the grace of the world bestowed upon him even at the last minute, in spite of the howling crowd that wanted Barabbas freed but not him.

But suicides die by their own choice. They alone could provide themselves with a saving grace and as soon as they reject it there is no further court of appeal to unabsolve them to go back to life. Now, as many different experiences in life and suicidology teach us very well, there is such a thing as the "ordeal-suicide," that kind of voluntary death in which a kind of divine judgment is invoked: suicidals choose a way of dying—preferably by taking sleeping pills—, through which the door remains ajar so that others can tear it open and bring them back to life. Many times Else G. took her veronal pills in a dosage carefully measured out to determine quantitatively, with certain variables, the probability of her exit. She gave life a chance of up to 70 percent. Her act was a game with fate up to the moment when she decided to settle the matter definitively. As long as the ordeal-suicide is not a clearly recognizable theatrical event staged to blackmail someone, so that the concept of suicide (or of attempted suicide) loses every justification and has to be taken back, the ordeal-suicide seems to me in its voluntary nature and its dignity to stand out from a silent suicide, from that letting-oneself-pass-away, as well as from death by martyrdom, including the death of the prophet on Golgotha. Those who lay hands on themselves are fundamentally different persons from those who surrender to the will of the others: with the latter something happens, the former act of their own accord. They set the time; they cannot count on acts of fate.

After the final conversations with oneself, which perhaps take place in front of the mirror where one chases after an already sentenced ego without catching it, only in order to take care of it again, the moment inexorably comes, the freely chosen moment, in which one lays hands on oneself. Something still more uncanny than the hunt for an ego enters here in various shapes: *time*. It's supposed to happen at nine in the evening—(according to statistics most suicides occur in the evening and early hours of night). At nine o'clock: now it is seven, thus twice sixty minutes for every sixty seconds. The second hand trots indefatigably; a minute's already gone, two, three, five, fifteen have passed away, you can smash the clock to pieces but can't turn off the gentle ticking of pure time. And in the time that still remains time is felt this way—whether there are hours, or only just minutes that one still grants oneself, this time is carried inside. It is only conditionally true what Freud says about the unconscious not knowing any time, about the way it orders events without chronological order, mixing them and turning them around. The passage of time is always present: in consciousness anyway, and it ticks as well in a metaphoric inner space stored deeper than all that is unconscious. For if it's true that the ego is world and space into which it throws itself and projects itself, then it is no less true that it is also time: the latter is more irredeemably fastened together with the subject than the space into which it strides to become both ego and world. It is the body that senses time.

This body-time has constantly been both relatively and absolutely irreversible. Relatively because the heartbeat repeated itself without remission, one breath following upon the other, sleep and waking relieving one another, again and again—so that one could even think that it would thus go on for all eternity. For years someone went in the summer to the same health resort, one July was like the other, one September looked like the same month the year before, the hotel room, for which reservations were carefully made early enough in advance, was the same. *Relatively* irreversible time made itself out as if it were not time, as if it could be turned around: in 1966 I visited the same place on the North Sea that I visited in 1972; the dates don't mean a thing. And in 1978, when I travel on the autobahn to the same place, it will be like it was in 1966. I repeat, the body knows better. It records, as a maliciously reliable registration apparatus, not only the years, the months, and the days, but every heartbeat, and none is identical with the previous one. With every stroke of the pump the heart wears itself down, the veins, kidneys, and eyes use themselves up. In moments of becoming abruptly and unexpectedly aware of one's frailty, experienced by everyone, humans know that they are creatures of time—for that they don't need to know anything about entropy. At some particular point the relatively irreversible time that we know from everyday experience—alas, tomorrow I have to do the same thing again, go the same way, see the familiar faces, and on throughout the year it will be the same—is experienced by mortals as absolutely irreversible.

Time: the form of perception of a faculty deep within us! But now the deep-within has emerged, at the top of my ego. Only one and a half hours more, a small eternity. A nothing. The body and the mind are now talking at once, the murmur of their voices can be heard in space. The body knows, in ninety minutes' time, the time it normally takes to reel off a movie, it will no longer be itself. It will smash on the asphalt, it will bleed until it stops bleeding, its central respiratory system will be abruptly paralyzed, or it will fall into a restless sleep that will change it forever. The body protests, even now, and will revolt even more savagely, as soon as its being is taken away from it. The mind—please let the simplifying everyday concepts pass, they intrude as soon as thinking reaches its limits—the mind gives orders.

And protests for itself against being taken out of time, and therefore against the fact that all the time layered up inside of it is disappearing. It recalls so much, everything has a temporal character because even space, which was not only the body's provenance but also the mind's, is now being bolted shut. It is voluntary death that puts an end to it, there is no escape and no hope, for in the name of dignity and as an answer to the *échec* the mental court of appeals itself offers its own extinction.

Absolute time, absolute since body and mind now know that no further deceptive repetitions will be organized, compresses itself on two levels. Memory, arrested in time, the memory of past times in the present, grabs its abundance closer and closer to itself until it is only a tiny, very heavy nucleus, a nucleus of the ego. So much has happened, and even in the most externally banal life. A draught of beer to cool the burning of the dried-out throat after a hike in the mountains. In damp weather the car started so badly, which one was it? The little red Modell Anglia, made in 1967. And now the compelling wish to jump back to that particular year. As in a dream, it is precisely those little events that assume such an inconceivable weight and temporal order, now, when the process of temporal compression becomes from second to second unbearable, like a burden, a mental burden, a bodily burden. *Le temps vécu*: the lived time is still present, even if enclosed within in the most minute proportions. But it will no longer be present, because its irreversibility is actualized and made concrete: it is not that death pursues the suicide, but that the suicide snatches it to his breast, closing tight all the doors through which help could enter. To paraphrase Hölderlin: where *this* danger is, rescue shrivels up.[8] When did I read him? Early in time, the precise date turns out to be immaterial, the feeling that it was *early* says enough. *Le temps vécu,* by Eugène Minkowski. When did I read that? Late. Probably around 1967. And the lateness speaks more clearly than any particular date. It is so late, so late, and well I know what's coming. Still another hour? Not a very long time. One could call everything off, get rid of the farewell letters and instructions for cremation that have already been prepared, start the car in front of the hotel, be able to cope again with the space we call world, and throw oneself into it. In order to suffer a new *échec* and yet another, again and again. No: here the highly private entropy will be completed and accelerated into madness. Three quarters of an hour more. Time is ticking on two levels and in two kinds of sound. It is now completely absolute—and it will be torn from its absoluteness and turned into nontime.

For Heidegger time is care. Put differently, the temporal "to" contains the characteristic of care in human existence, of taking care of, of providing care. One who lays hands on oneself does not have, as it must be, any care anymore and, along with that, has no time. On the other hand, however, one experiences for oneself, precisely because one "has no time"—whose limits are already set by the will to make an end—that time is more peculiar to one than ever. With each forward movement of the second hand time becomes thicker and heavier. One has more and more time to the degree that one's own commandment leaves one less time. Thus one has more and more ego, but only as a perpetually insoluble riddle, because, blind and unruly in the haste of the chase, one knows, the closer one tries to press it to oneself, that much less of what to do with it. Time is stored in the ego, it fills it up with fear of the hour hand's pace, lies heavily in the body that wants to ward it off, unconditionally demanding to *be*, even though prohibited from doing so by just that mind that itself would like to last and has forbidden it to itself. Maybe even not caring is just an illusion. Twenty minutes more. The world is ultimately still always present, even if it is not allowed to be any more. The fear is great. Smashing and cracking. Floods falling over the head, the mouth of which will perhaps cry for help against the commandment of the mind. The effect of sleeping pills. On the table, things to attend to have been placed in painstaking order. Reeling from the table to the bed. One could fall down, tearing the telephone receiver from the rest of the apparatus, it is so easy to get caught in the cord. And the night porter would check to see if everything is in order. Sirens, an ambulance. *Just in case,* one needs to ensure that none of that happens. Recent research in the field of theoretical physics has, beyond the objective space-time continuum, even beyond thermodynamics, defined a concept of time according to which time once *began*—something nobody can completely contemplate. And much too strange to contest and debate. To lay hands on oneself is in a murderous way—*Selbstmord* is good here; for once this nasty word fits—to rule over time as well as to serve it, one's own time, the only time one still wants to know about, because now one finds oneself in the condition of total ipseity. What is woman to me, what is child to me; what do physics and objective knowledge, what does the fate of a world that will sink away with me matter to me? Time concentrates and presses itself together in an ego that does not have itself.

The world as temporality pushes the world of space out of the pit in which the ego is concealed. Whoever lays hands on oneself does not have another chance to take hold of anything other than expired time, to get anywhere else than to the rubble field of one's own historicity, which itself is growing more and more unfounded as more and more objects or ruins of objects pile themselves up. These things do not establish any further resistance for the subject; it is no longer impelled to cope with them. —And how many minutes are left?

But the dice are not yet cast. Maybe ten more minutes that one apportions to oneself. These minutes still let themselves stretch out into a deceptive eternity. Having already chosen to die, one is beset by the sweet enticement of life and its logic right up to the last second. The necrophiliac tenderness for the dying body can easily be converted into the redeeming decision to cancel the undertaking so that a cosmic tenderness would emerge in place of disgust and the inclination to death. The absolute irreversibility of time could still be relativized: today just as yesterday and the day before yesterday, tomorrow as well as the day after tomorrow, the heart would beat, one beat would be deceptively like the other, an awakening would appear like so many past and eternally future awakenings. A trick of a prestidigitator, whose stupendous manual skill appears before our half-witted staring eyes to accomplish the impossible.

Mais déjà le couperet va tomber, d'un instant à l'autre (But the blade is going to fall, at any instant now), the executioner is not idle. Now it's just a question of what we call dignity: someone who is suicidal is determined to be a suicide, and never again to trust ridiculously everyday life and its alienation or the wisdom of the psychologists or their partners, who will certainly breathe in again with relief and will scarcely be able to suppress a forgiving smile. And so it would happen and so it does happen, in whatever way. Dignity sets the flares. Failing would be the most unforgivable and unforgettable disgrace, a further *échec* that would necessarily introduce a series of even more of these. The second hand trots relentlessly toward the minute of truth. The act is set in motion. Outside of the ego, enclosed in itself and perhaps finding its nucleus at the end, no one else will be able to assess this act. The world's objectivity will try to dissect it: it will only be dead tissue, which practiced hands and brains will reduce to pulp with as much industry as futility.

IV. Belonging to Oneself

Someone who sets about to try to grasp the idea of voluntary death, even if only for an hour, even if only flirtatiously and playfully, will only poorly understand society's obtrusive solicitude for his final fate. It has, this society, never troubled itself very much about his existence and what it is like. War is concocted: he will be called up and charged with proving his worth in the midst of blood and iron. Society took his work from him after it raised him for it: now he is unemployed, he is sent packing with alms that he consumes as he consumes himself with them. He gets sick: but unfortunately there are not enough hospital beds, the expensive palliatives are rare and the most expensive of all, a single room, is not made available to him. Not until now, when he wishes to give in to the inclination toward death, when he is no longer willing to offer any resistance to his disgust with being, when dignity and humanity order him to dispose of the matter neatly and to achieve what he one day will have to achieve anyway: to disappear—only now does society behave as if he were its most precious part and surround him with hideous equipment, parading before him the highly repulsive occupational ambition of physicians who can then ascribe his "rescue" to the credit side of their professional account like hunters when they pace off the spot where their game was slaughtered. In their opinion, they have retrieved him from death and they behave like sportsmen who have succeeded in an extraordinary achievement.

No doubt, there's something funny about this. I mean on the one hand the cold indifference society displays toward individual human beings and its heated-up care for one of them who wants to step voluntarily out of association with the living. Is each person its property? Here and there I have already rejected by implication the demand society makes on those ready for death. Here the question needs to be asked once again and then answered: *To whom does a human being belong?*

The first to feel the need to interfere in all this are believing Christians. They know for certain that humans belong to the Lord to whom they owe their lives and whose privilege it is to take their lives from them when it's suitable to Him. I don't have anything to say to those who decide for themselves on their own to obey and to belong to (the two words in German have a close etymological relationship!) their God. The philosopher Paul Ludwig Landsberg, of Jewish blood and Christian faith, carried poison with him as an emigrant in France pursued by the German occupying forces and their French collaborators in order to escape the compulsory death of the executioners in voluntary death. "It is certain," reports the philosopher Arnold Metzger, a pupil of

Scheler and Husserl who edited Landsberg's posthumous writings,[1] "that he destroyed the poison in the summer of 1942. When he was arrested, he was no longer willing to have his own life at his disposal. He was living what he thought." And as a creature and servant of his God he went into that death that other children of his God, the brown-shirted executioners, prepared for him in Oranienburg; how, I don't want to know at all. The man deserves my highest respect and he has it, even though I'd rather hear about those who struck down at least one of the flunkies who came to get them. In any case, our high respect for this man of God should be expressed and affirmed. But it ends, in my eyes, when the philosopher becomes concerned not only with himself and his destiny, but wants to be heard as one who proclaims the word of God in the company of others and as one who in the name of his Lord makes demands on them. For in a remarkably profound essay about "The Moral Problem of Suicide," he wrote these words: "We surely have the right, if we would like to die, to ask God to let us die; but always with the addition: thy will be done, not mine. Yet this God is not our Lord as a lord of slaves: he is our father. He is the Christian God who loves us eternally and with eternal wisdom. If He lets us suffer, then it is for our salvation, for our purification."

I protest as vehemently and as emphatically as I can. If this unhappy man I've quoted made no use of the possibilities available to him for killing himself and surrendered to the death his executioners were preparing for him (a martyr's death?—maybe; but in my opinion the sacrifice of his life in preference to the human dignity of a voluntary death!), then this was entirely his business. His words about the Christian

God who "loves us with eternal wisdom" as He delivers us to trampling boots or a fiery oven are in my eyes truly blasphemous. The man had every right to be his own person and as such to offer himself to his God as a victim; but it borders on inhumanity when he elevates this, his personal decision, only valid for him, to an imperative to surrender to something that is for others a phantasm. Everyone has the right to be one's own person in submission to a God that one imagines—in the end even self-sacrifice to the idea of humanity is also probably nothing more than an illusion. But no one has the right to dictate to others in which way, and with regard to whatever, they realize what is their own in life and death.

It has to be said right away that the claim of religion on the individual human being, as soon as we establish the relationship to voluntary death, is of the same nature as the demand of society: neither the latter nor the former permit one the freedom to decide how to deal with what one possesses in fact and law. Both demand of individuals (and just think here of Kant who, as a consequence of his categorical idea of duty, rejected voluntary death just as much as any little village pastor or great theologian) that they relinquish their freedom of choice: not voluntarily, but in obedience to a duty to God or to humanity. The religious hold on human beings is nothing other than the expression of a hold that is social and, if in former times the churches denied Christian burial to suicides, their actions were no different from those of primitive tribes for whom the cadaver of a suicide is in possession of something unclean that has to be removed from the living as quickly as possible in order to stave off evil spirits. But even those social units that tolerate suicide, and under circumstances even make it a duty, such as the more tightly knit social organization of the Japanese warrior caste, understand it as a social phenomenon and interpret it in the sense of preserving the species or the continuation of the social organization in question. As far as I can see, voluntary death—with the quantitatively negligible exceptions of philosophical schools or philosophizing individuals (Epicurus, Seneca, Diderot)—is nowhere recognized for what it is: a precisely *free and voluntary* death and a highly individual matter that, to be sure, is never carried out without social reference, with which however and finally *human beings are alone with themselves, before which society has to be silent.*

It is apparent to me that we're still not beyond that inhuman, spiritual stage of development that covers suicide with anathema. Except that where religious commandments and prohibitions used to require that voluntary death be viewed as a crime or where the social order was so lacking in shame (but still honest enough) to confess that it was only concerned with human beings as *material*, with human working power, so that consequently potential suicides of the slave class were frightened away from their plans by terrifying threats of punishment, today it is sociology, psychiatry, and psychology that are the appointed bearers of public order, that deal with voluntary death as one deals with a sickness. In this socially bound outlook all suicidological theories are fundamentally united with each other. Those whom they call potential "self-murderers" must be hindered from constituting themselves in voluntary death. Life is the only good: it has to be preserved and it makes no difference now whether it should be preserved because

God gave it or because this life itself as a social phenomenon has been assigned a quasi-metaphysical value, one that
in truth is biological and as such is both confirmed (human
beings are born) and denied (they die off) everywhere and
every day.

As I am putting these lines on paper, about thirty doctors are diabolically at work, medically abusing the Spanish
dictator Francisco Franco, who has become a rasping skel-
eton, so that a life that for weeks has borne no resemblance
to life at all can be extended for a few hours or days. I have,
and always have had, the greatest antipathy for this cruel,
even bloodthirsty man. But at this moment it is unbearable
to me to learn how doctors, intoxicated by their technol-
ogy, debase themselves. I would like to call out to them,
"Stop! Do you want to be as inhuman as the victim of your
nightmarish butchery and depraved instrumental precision?"
We shouldn't try to compare things that are incommensurable. The hard-working theoreticians and practitioners of
suicidology and suicide-prophylaxis have nothing to do with
the busy implantation of pacemakers and the cadaver-engi-
neers at Franco's bed who are armed with syringes and tubes.
But it was probably not by chance that in the midst of dealing with problems of voluntary death such a connection of
ideas presented itself to me. For no matter how one always
views it, no matter how much one recognizes the human
impulse of the affected researchers and practitioners, there
still remains on the side of society in its prevailing system of
values something violent and hostile, not only in the reani-
mation of an attempted suicide but even in the principled
ostracism of the act itself, whether it is carried out or pre-
vented. The ancient idea of *sin* still haunts research on the

subject. The Viennese suicidologist Erwin Ringel talks of the "defective development" that leads to suicide or attempted suicide, without considering that the formation of such a concept emanates from the premise that suicide is, and must be, a mistake, without seriously taking into account that those with "defective development" and with psychological preconditions like those of potential suicides do not in the overwhelming majority come to a decision to commit suicide, and frequently do not even sustain any particular psychic damage. Another researcher, Erwin Stengel, investigates the appeal-characteristic of voluntary death, viewing it as the last desperate cry for help of a potential or actual suicide, a wildly propelled cry into the wildness of the world: "Help me, I can't go on!" The thesis has much going for it and later I want to try to argue about it. Meanwhile let me just say that even Stengel does not try to understand those who are determined to take their own lives from the standpoint of their own world. To be sure, voluntary death is almost always an appeal, in addition to whatever else it is, or as I prefer to call it, a *message*. But beyond this it is something totally different, specifically something that we can still speak about only metaphorically or in some kind of empty conceptual poetry, the ending of a condition without which no way of being a condition is even possible, the ending of life, an act that cannot be reversed, an excessive action that turns everyone who hears of it pale.

Not everything suggested to us in psychological theories can be false. But they always *miss the mark* of the fundamental fact that *each human being essentially belongs to himself or herself*—outside of the network of social entanglements, outside of the network of a biological destiny and prejudgment that condemns one to life. To the unbiased glance of an observer who is not devoted to orthodoxy, the "classical" psychoanalytic theory seems more like a desperate attempt to rescue an entire thought structure that excludes suicide in its basic premises than to be a serious method of dealing with a person who is suicidal. We know the mechanism: the libido that is invested in an object becomes available as soon as this object—a person, an idea—is lost; instead of turning to another object, however, it withdraws into the ego, and henceforth becomes a part of it. The object that has been lost is certainly saved in this way, but from now on its hate, the conversion of disappointed or lost love, is directed against the internalized object and therefore against the ego, its own person, which must therefore be destroyed. I cannot make a judgment about the extent to which clinical experiences may appear as verification of their ideas to those adept in the art of psychoanalysis. For their part, these experiences are as such questionable because they are still not pure experience, but have instead a pattern, the classic theoretical model, as their basis. For the *phenomenological* eye, the phenomenon of suicide is a *quantité négligeable*, or, to say it more plainly, a far-fetched construction dragged in by the hair. The theory boils down to the manifestations of auto-aggression, which the psychoanalyst Karl Menninger later designated as a function of the death and destruction instinct and worked out in his book *Man against Himself* by drawing upon numerous case histories. I have already discussed the concept of the death instinct in an earlier chapter, where I suggested the less ostentatious expression, "inclination toward death." I'd only like to append at this point, in light of an intuition unrestrained by theory, that to commit aggression against another and to lay hands on oneself are two radically different ways of acting. It is simply incorrect to say that the act that is always erroneously called "self-murder" in German is nothing else but a substitution for murder. The murder of a fellow creature is the most extreme form of confirming one's own *life*. Here Elias Canetti, with his anthropologically imagined concept of the *triumphant survivor* that is well beyond psychology, has interpreted the circumstances of the killing of another in a way that corresponds to the act itself, I have no doubt about that.[2] The act of laying hands on myself, to the point of death or just to that of self-mutilation, is in the phenomenal space of the ego to speak a language of particular meaning that is different from that of murder. I take hold of something: my extremities are directed away from me, in the world or against the world (the Latin word "in," used to mean "notwithstanding," makes the facts of this case extremely clear).

I take hold of myself *myself*, and carry out an exercise that in the daily practice of life only occurs when I want to remove or get rid of something alien and disturbing; this exercise is an event of an incomparably different order. I brush my teeth, I clean my ears, my nose: reestablish my *physis* in its integrity. That is not actually a seizing of myself, but an aggression against the outside world, which in any case is hostile, which I have to hold far from me in order to exist, to endure. Auto-aggression seems to me to be a logically nonsensical concept, more exactly stated: a concept that only in the framework of the anti-logic of death gains justification, whereby it must lose everything that is aggressive *in a positive sense*, which according to the findings of

behavioral researchers makes the indispensable readiness
for life obvious. Here, everyday language is a reliable guide
through the labyrinth of the breast.[3] "An aggressive businessman": that certainly describes a successful merchant,
fit for life, and the exact opposite of a person who yields to
an inborn inclination toward death and even violently re-
claims it for himself and pulls the "dear brother death," about
whom Hermann Hesse speaks in one of his few good po-
ems,[4] impatiently to his breast.

But what's the point of this ill-mannered tone that forces
itself against psychological theories of suicide? I have to forbid it to myself on the spot because I realize all too well that
I am already partly talking in that other language, the language of suicides; these doctrines are no more capable of
reaching them than the sociological strivings of a Durkheim,
of someone half awake, or of all those who think that it is
not individuals who give themselves an independent death,
but society in its problematic nature that leads each separate person, poorly armed, without resistance, and at its
mercy, to suicide. What I am aiming at is just the crucial
point at which it becomes apparent that all suicide research,
the psychological and the sociological, speaks in the name
of society—even when it most sharply criticizes the prevailing social order!—instead of looking for potential suicides
in the only place where they can be found: in each one's
own inalienable system. For (I repeat this even though I
know I am in danger of wearying the reader and bringing
upon myself an accusation of monotony) everyone belongs
at the decisive moments of one's life to oneself, and when
one no longer wants to belong to oneself because of submitting to an idea, to a human association, to a delusion, it

doesn't matter what, it is still an existential act of belonging to oneself that makes one act or not act.

Obviously, this is taking me into the field of ethics against my intention. I don't like to do it because in such circumstances one can all too quickly develop a liability and be taken into custody as an outsider. Society is the summing up of individuals, but in this summation it transcends the vital facts of subjectivity. But it has its rights, rights that in the end revert to the benefit of the individual. And no one is permitted to withdraw oneself completely from certain total claims of society. It is therefore not possible for a person with a moral sensibility to bring about his or her voluntary death in a way that endangers the lives of others, such as using a car in so wild a rage that it could crash into other vehicles and physically harm their occupants or even only cause material damages. Here it is necessary to stick to the logic of life in the form of ethical principles, right up to the end and against the logic of death and "*après moi, le déluge.*" Which, by the way, even happens in most cases, as far as the suicidological literature I've seen indicates. I've never read of a pilot or an engineer of a locomotive, determined to take his own life, who has taken the passengers who are in his trust with him into his own death. In contradiction to that, the criminal phenomenon of a murder followed by suicide is relatively common, as in the *crime passionel* when a jealous man does away with his unfaithful lover and then himself. The immanent logic of suicide permits no justifiable exculpation for such actions. Just the same, I think that we have to keep two things apart here: murder (that is, an act committed by many without afterwards laying hands on themselves) and suicide. Murderers are murderers; their crime is a crime. That beyond their criminal act they may kill themselves does not wipe away their atrocity, nor does it make them double criminals. As the murderers that they were they should not be morally pardoned. As suicides, standing before us as such, they have settled their affairs: they stand beyond judgment and pardon, persons whose right over their own life, their death, may not be impugned. The scale of cases in which ethical problems intrude into suicidal situations stretches out over a great distance, too great for us to be able to analyze every single nuance. Let us only ask, as an example, about the man who, as it is society's will, has a responsibility to his family to continue to live. He is the provider: he has to keep providing, keep supplying the cursed fodder for a voracious family pack that doesn't want to see the shadow of death over his head and on his brow, but greedily demands love and tenderness and care and defense and responsibility. Does he have to acquiesce and give in? Is it his duty to live for the others? Moral dispositions in such cases will proceed with care and give fundamental ethical principles their due. A man, let us assume, who is trying to die and who is looking for death, has a sick, unemployable spouse and two young children. Viewed ethically and without consideration of psychological factors, he must understand how to control his inclination toward death. Such cases are rare among the suicides reported by the relevant research. But almost everywhere, when someone departs from us or is taken away, we see with insistent clarity *how little a human being matters.*

As a member of the Academy of the Arts in Berlin, twice a year I have the opportunity to hear the obituaries for deceased members of the institution and to participate in the ritual "minute of silence" in honor of the dead. Everyone actually stands at a kind of attention for about sixty seconds and then sits down again, relieved after this awkwardness. The obituaries are read aloud. For the most part only those who read them actually listen with attention. The others look at their fingernails and doodle on the notepads lying in front of them. After the suicide of Peter Szondi, after Ingeborg Bachmann's horrible death,[5] there was also some talk. It sure straightened things out. And the survivors concentrated on such urgent problems as the allocation of prizes or the election of new members. But those are strangers, someone will object. Think of how different the reactions of close friends are, especially family members. Of course. But they, too, forget with a stupendous rapidity. The widows soon laugh again—why shouldn't they? The widowers comfort themselves with other ladies. For the children, papa soon becomes a myth that people remember with that kind of boredom that attacks one in religious classes. *Les absents ont toujours tort: les morts ont doublement tort et sont plus morts que mort* (The absent are always wrong: the dead are doubly wrong and are deader than dead). Death is more than death: the funeral banquet that gets rid of it is the great act of cleaning up carried out by the living to remove the filth of death. Disregarding a few extreme cases such as those introduced above, potential suicides know that they are permitted to obey themselves, that they belong to themselves, that they die their death, their own, not one that the Lord first needs to give to them. They are all alone with their voluntary death, alone as they would be with a "natural" demise. They must be aware of that.

Except that with such knowledge a quite definite aspect

of suicide comes into the twilight. With it we return to the discussion of suicidological theories. Isn't voluntary death a cry for help, as Erwin Stengel declares in his book, *Suicide and Attempted Suicide*? "Help me, I can't go on," or something like that. I prefer speaking of a *message*, as I've already said, and am trying now to elucidate an intricate set of circumstances. To be sure, it seems to me that this "appeal" not only exists but that many suicides or attempted suicides actually may be viewed as a cry out of the night of an inimical state of being, just as there are also such things as the pure blackmail-suicide, the revenge-suicide, the shameless theatrical demonstration of the pseudo-suicide, planned from the beginning as "unsuccessful." With a hysterical cry, a woman in the presence of her husband, and perhaps even other persons, runs to the window and assures those present that she intends to jump. That is lamentable, though hardly ridiculous, for we dare not laugh about any human misery. A man who annihilates himself writes before setting about the deed, "You have tortured me, I cannot bear it any longer, so now the guilt is yours." Or only: "Now I have to go, everything I tried was rejected, I am turning my back on the world that expelled me." We know all these things and psychology can find the proper way to interpret the special cases. That is not what interests me. What conceptually unites all plans for voluntary death, those that succeed in the end as well as those that result in recalling the departure, is not the cry for help but the *message*. This message, which does not have to be written down, cried out, defined by any kind of sign, but is instead given along the way in the silent act, means that we ourselves at the moment of stepping over the line, when we have already issued our refusal to the logic of life and the demands of being, still have in a part of our person something to do with the *other*, right up to the last flicker of our consciousness. As we know, the other is "hell":[6] my freedom is frustrated by that of the other, the other's project stands in the way of mine, the other's subjectivity intends to annihilate mine, already the glance of the other alone, which sets me right and condemns me to a particular way of being, is a kind of murder. In my meeting with the other something happens to me that Sartre calls *la chute originelle*, the original fall or plunge. This is true, but not entirely. Because the other, with his glance, his project, his fixing of my ego, is both murderer *and Samaritan*. The other is the breast of my mother and the helpful hand of a nurse. The other is more: the "you"; specifically, without which I could never be an "I." What we do, what we leave undone is always in hate, in passion, in friendship, and even in indifference related to the other. We can get along without God. We can't manage without the other. We like to call it "society," but that is only a question of conventional terminology. As our destiny, the other, as good or bad as our ego, and once again just like our ego, is our companion to the end. Alvarez tells us in his book *The Savage God* the frightening story of a decidedly Anglophiliac American residing in England, who, in a flawless "city gentleman's" suit, with a bowler hat and a neatly rolled umbrella, after taking a sufficient dose of sleeping pills, jammed himself into a crevice in a cliff on the coast, turned toward his American native land, and there died. The message was clear and was also independent of the specific psychological motivation of the suicide. It was: I love England and I love my native land. Both countries stood here as representatives for the other to whom the sign was directed. And even where clear signs are lacking, a message is sent out. Then perhaps the other, who does not have a face anymore, is not a country, friend, or lover, becomes a transcendental object. The other's presence only ends with the death of the suicide; he, she, or it is the addressee of the message. Whether the message arrives or not cannot in general be answered. If it is a direct message addressed vengefully to an unfaithful lover, its chances of arriving are slight. The report of the man that can be expressed in the words, "See what you have caused!" will be but a small burden of conscience and a great relief. Because the loved one of yesterday is no longer such a one today, because as a lover he had no right to life and to messages; the unwritten letter will not be accepted, the cry will not be heard. This number is out of service, this number is out of service. But if the message is a universally abstract one and addressed to the other as a mere figure of speech for that state of being from which the suicide wants to escape, the broken record will continue with increased emphasis and just a slightly varied text: your call cannot be completed as dialed, cannot be completed, cannot be completed.

None of this should matter to any of those who are getting ready to dispatch themselves. But it is the confounded and deplorable case that, in the way things are, suicides are just as incapable of disregarding the other as anyone who leads a carefree existence. A man has already said adieu, he knows that he will not see anyone again. Nevertheless, in parting he calls over his shoulder to the other a word that makes no sense: not only because it's never certain that it gets to anyone's ear, but, and above all, because as he withdraws he will not know anything about it. And with this the whole problem of subjective idealism in philosophy, long since laid aside, as one would like to think, presents itself anew and in another light. The world is my idea. The other was my idea. With the extinction of my ego, the idea is extinguished, world and others are all gone. Suicides try to carry this out with a balancing act of thinking that ends with the acrobat's fall but doesn't entirely carry it out. With their deed they address the other: the other passes away with them and remains in existence. They make their appeal exactly as if they were as thoroughly convinced of the disappearance of the "world in one's head" as they were of its continuing. Each suicide is Tom Sawyer who cries at his own grave with his fellow human beings and nevertheless knows that he won't have any more tears. In this contradiction, death is really *le faux*, the false, the perverted, of which Sartre speaks: and is in spite of that the only truth that, like the God of the faithful, encompasses all contradictions in itself and cancels them in its embrace. So suicides kill themselves, together with the other whom they address with a message. So they let the world perish that, whether their "idea" or not, was their possession. In the consciousness of a suicide the absurdity is run to death that one belongs to oneself and, in belonging to oneself, also belongs to the world; *that the world belongs to one* and thereby one to oneself. There is no profounder proposition than Wittgenstein's statement that stands as a motto at the beginning of this book, in which the philosopher of positive thinking surrenders himself, becomes an existential thinker or nonthinker, and does not shy away from a series of words that his followers will calmly designate as "senseless." "The world of the happy person is a different one from that of the unhappy person. Just as with death the world does not change, but stops." With the stopping of the world by death the fact that suicides belong to themselves is confirmed. And the dispatched message, which they can't forbid themselves, resounds in the nonworld of death.

If, along with Erwin Stengel, we speak of the "appeal-characteristic" of voluntary death, then we find ourselves again in the space of the world of psychology. If we also recognize this appeal-function's contradictory nature, one that is not only immanent, but transcendent, even perhaps transcendental, then we have left the realm of psychology (a science of the living, in title if not in objective fact) and stand in the half-darkness of ontological speculation. But we will not go one more step further! For already the false, cold light of metaphysical construction is breaking in, already our mind is being illuminated in a highly deceiving and probably cheap way by the empty conceptuality of subjective idealism, which we must reject. The world, as Wittgenstein said, stops with death, but no one ultimately doubts de facto that it continues to be and un-be until entropy prepares an end for it that is understandable to human reason. Someone will bury our remains, burn them, dissect them. Streetcars and airplanes will continue to perform their service, men and women will pair off and call forth new unreasonable demands in their moans of pleasure—or without pleasure in a middle-class marital way. Better than those who depart in a "natural way," hankering after improvement and appreciation and shoving death from themselves, suicides know both the perishing of the world and its continued existence. As a phenomenon, each suicide is as rare as a genius, even if one is only a poor dog for whom no one will shed a tear. But suicides are also the only ones among the far too many who, sending a message into the void, *understand the world*: as people who only belong to themselves and are resolute opponents of everything that is called reality in everyday language and scientific expression.

To allege something like this is to expose oneself to the danger of accusations of verbal intemperance and a licentious attempt to be intellectually provocative. How reasonable the theories are in contrast. They spread factual material out before us, classify it, and make known the utterances of re-awakened attempted suicides. Among the many doctrinal opinions (which know no more about suicide than a mechanic who knows every component part of a car but doesn't know anything about the physical laws of motion) there is one that is particularly striking to us. What is suicide? A "narcissistic crisis." A representative of this theory writes, "If one separates the critical inception of the fixation on the problem from its ultimate objectivization and also directs it to other steps of scientific knowledge, e.g. to the process of forming hypotheses, it might be possible to develop a more adequate access to the phenomenon of suicidality."

He directs the inception to steps and develops access. What's going on? Not everyone writes like Freud and these clumsy words are not necessarily a judgment about the thought behind them, except that in this case what is being thought is carried out in ridiculous disproportion to the horrifying event. However, it certainly does not appear any more disproportionate than a technical surgical treatise about the inhuman process of an amputation. These things have to be dispassionate. One has to tell oneself that amputations are necessary and theoretical reports about them are unavoidably necessary as well; and there are suicide cases, and research reports about them, too. They don't lose their value because of their clumsy language. So we'll let researchers use their language as they have developed it and we'll only inquire about the results of their work, which finally, produced as they usually are, have a certain technical relationship to our discourse.

Voluntary death, so it is claimed, is a narcissistic crisis. Technically bypassing the problems of concept formation I should only incidentally mention that I am not comfortable with such nomenclature but I recognize that that is my problem. I do not think one should talk of narcissism without being mentally clear—or acknowledging one's lack of clarity—about the ego and its relation to itself. Let it also be noted that it is surely a misuse of the expression "sadism" to use it without expressly meaning sexual pleasure in causing physical pain and that the word masochism should not be allowed unless we have in view cases in which someone goes into ecstasy merely over the idea of being abused. Let us put these terminological questions aside and confine ourselves to the essence of the utterance. Suicide, according to a particular line of research, has nothing to do with Freud's disputed death instinct, nothing to do with the object-cathexis and internalization of the object that, as something to be hated, eventually becomes part of the subject that begets the self-hatred that leads to "self-murder." Instead, it is supposed to behave in such a way that a potential suicide, disappointed by the behavior of others with respect to him, can no longer love himself in the mirror that the others are for him. The poor devil has constructed an ego "alien to reality": reality reflected back to him a different image of his person, one that was not gratifying to him. "A narcissistic object-relationship" led to "frustration," so he killed himself, as a mentally disturbed person.

This casuistical construction has much going for it, probably more, and with deeper import, than its authors can dream. We only need to omit the unhappy expression "narcissism"—and of course "object-relationship" and more obviously "frustration"—and we suddenly find ourselves confronting a terrifying phenomenon, about which we have already talked: the "other," as my mirror—but even more as adversary and "hell"—stands in my way. Here there are no social theories that can help. The other wants me as it wants me. I *never* correspond to this will, no matter how friendly, how well-disposed and full of fellow-feeling, it may show itself to be. I am alone, even without being "socially isolated." Loneliness is not abandonment, at least not fundamentally and in every case. One can be profoundly alone in the midst of a pressing crowd, can be radiated with fame, and be aware of being surrounded by honors and by people paying homage and nevertheless have a feeling of being totally alone. When someone emerges from the depths of such despair and makes a decision for voluntary death, is it therefore to be diagnosed as a "narcissistic crisis"? Or isn't it instead the case that, after slowly preparing the way, potential suicides grasp the knowledge that we are isolated, no matter how many companions we may also have? "No one can be a companion to anyone here," it is said.[7] But it is questionable what use the love of the other is to me. At the

great colloquium organized by the psychoanalytic movement in 1910 on the theme of "self-murder," one of the
participants got up and proclaimed, "The only kind of person who chooses death is someone who has no more hope
for love." Only such a person? Really? As far as its clinical
and statistical documentation is concerned, the statement
hangs in the void. We don't know at all if people do themselves in solely and only because of the (authentic or imaginary) lack of the love of others. Just as we don't know how
many have done it because they could not bear the burden
of love heaped upon them. The wrong love at the wrong
time from the wrong other can just as easily lead to suicide
as a lack of demonstrated love. What we can speak of with
justified conviction is only the *existential loneliness of the individual*: that knowledge is given to us directly at every hour
of the day. And likewise we are given a twofold feeling of
being delivered into the hands of the other who passes judgment on us and the need for an other on whom we may
pass judgment. But this other, understood here as a transcendental object, does not have to assume the tangible
shape of a definite human being. It can hide itself behind
"world" without being therefore less present to us. In saying this, I do not exclude that on the level of the theories of
psychological motivation people who are socially isolated
actually seek death more frequently than those who are
called "well-integrated." In any case the statistics attest to
this even though their validity is of course called into question by many suicidologists, such as the American J. D. Doug-
las, who took it upon himself to throw all statistical method-
ology overboard, including Durkheim's monumental work.
But if we ourselves want to trust the generally accepted facts

and figures and on their basis assume that people standing alone would more likely give themselves over to the inclination toward death than those fixed in a definite place in a social system, this still does not say anything about the *fundamental condition of loneliness* of the subject, projected into a hostile world and steadily basing itself on the other while just as permanently being destroyed by that very other.

A man goes home in the evening and says to himself in the poorly lighted street he has to cross: nothing is worth anything, my trouble is not worth anything, what I could hope for is an illusion that consumes itself in its realization. I am going to make an end to this wretched business. But just then someone at home talks about what's for dinner and about having a cold and about tomorrow's weather. Just now suicidal, he is inundated by everyday life, swims along in the dreary water, and never even gets to his loneliness as a complete experience, becoming still more wretched and miserable. He is worse off than a fellow creature who goes home at the same hour with the same ideas who doesn't find any idle talk that alienates him from himself. Everything was useless, this second man says, and it won't be worth anything tomorrow and every other day. Let's make an end to it all. Next morning a neighbor finds his cadaver. He belonged to himself and he obeyed himself. To the psychological facts that, expressed or not, presuppose life as *value* he responded with his own decision, measured out only for him. He didn't cancel the facts out by that, but now they are illuminated differently. Naturally, his act—it is an act in comparison to the nonact of those who let themselves be flushed away by everyday life and idle talk—is still a message, for he too, alone and perhaps free, cannot manage without the other. But what does it mean when someone calls his action the result of a "narcissistic crisis?" He isn't trying to make the world throw back to him a flattering mirror image of his self. On the contrary: he doesn't want to see the mirror image that, friendly or not, is a caricature of his ego. In my eyes, the validity of this state of affairs is absolutely universal, though I have no means of "proving" it (and incidentally I'd like to note that the "human sciences" can never in the strict sense advance their propositions as proven facts).

I generally think—to carry this line of thought a bit further—that no one "loves oneself" (understood in the same sense as when one loves another) so little that one's ego-condition makes it permissible to hate oneself. One's ego, our ego, is only in a limited measure and in a superficial way capable of stepping outside of itself: it is continually necessary to see oneself, love oneself, and hate oneself in a mediated way by always furtively internalizing, until recalled, a look that enters one's awareness through language (verbally or in some other semiotic way). People look for their ego as a transcendental object only in the rarest and most absorbed moments, and even then they don't find it— as I've already shown. Whatever one loves or hates is the piece of the world that one has stridently made to be one's own: moments of exaltation, preserved within, and situations of humiliation that weigh more stubbornly upon one, in spite of all mechanisms of suppression and defense. The most miserable existence still has its moments of honor. In one case, it may have been the day of confirmation, in another a morning in landscapes that deceptively promise happiness, here a new erotic experience, there only a drifting scrap of music or a few lines of poetry. They were and are in the memory. They will no longer be. No one will carry them on as world into the sad world of death. Even when disgust predominates and the inclination to death overpowers us. One's own body, of which I spoke in the third section, the tenderness for it, going beyond the voluntary death I have in mind to excruciating necrophilia, is in the last analysis the physical body of my being-in-the-world, and if I stroke my right hand with my left, the left with the right, both together like lovers—then they are the parts of my body in which world has sheltered itself. Inner world? Outer world? The question becomes superfluous. To be correct, it has to be called *experienced* world, *monde vécu, temps vécu, espace vécu* (lived world, lived time, lived space). Lived. To hold oneself to the lived has no *tertium comparationis* with narcissism, insofar as we want to get involved with this concept at all. Everyone is narcissistic. No one is. Precisely because everyone is. The simplest language says that our shirt is closer to us than our coat—and it is right in its parsimonious simplicity. —And our skin is even closer than our shirt and our stratified world-in-us still much closer than even our skin. It is entirely ours, in our miseries as well as in our glories, and we belong to it, meaning: we belong to ourselves.

It should be explained right away that society, which sets itself up against us with its presumptions and unwarranted expectations, is not our world but only the material for it. A society, and that means every single one of them, is, in opposition to me, a multitude of accomplishments made by others and by me, but in such a manner that my own accomplishments in it are just as foreign to me as those of my co-players. I can take something from this material and make it a part of my person. Something else I can reject, no matter how violently it may also beset me. Only what I've soaked up is essential, the rest is horrible excrement. In completing the process of getting rid of what is repulsive, am I renouncing the reality-principle whose binding force is universal? One may just as well declare: I have never completely possessed the reality-principle, even if, not being insane, I obviously accommodated myself to it.

Here I want to draw a radical line of demarcation between my considerations and certain anti-psychiatric theories that reject the reality-principle as an instrument of oppression of a specific social order. The equation "reality = capitalistic oppression" is false. More likely, it is true that society *as* society is always right against us just as we, as individuals, are in all circumstances right against it. The contradiction is resolved only with the dissolution or salvation of our existence. "Reality," the balance of the innumerable ideas, mediated by language, that succeed in being uttered and therefore in being intersubjective, cannot be dismissed. Themistocles was an Athenian general; so it is said and so it *is*. Whoever would try to be heard with the statement, "Themistocles is my iron," would be viewed first as a joker and, if he stubbornly repeated it, as a fool. Whatever the word "Themistocles" means for the subject—perhaps something starlike, perhaps a thundering sound, or even actually the heat of the iron—that is the subject's own and it is incommunicable, there's nothing to make of that. In other words, those who are "normal" will link themselves to the generally valid meaning conveyed to them, so that the word indicates, "means," an Athenian general—without reflecting further about what "meaning" means. It is, yet again, the "other," cutting a figure here in the concept of a sociality transmitted in language that asserts itself victoriously against an ego. This ego must only then be "disturbed" when it maintains an intimate relationship to the word Themistocles that has nothing to do with accepting the fact that here an Athenian general is being discussed.

A suicide, who can be disturbed but does not *per definitionem* have to be, does not yet definitively break his pact with reality. He adheres to the contract even though he thoroughly accedes to the certainty that contracts are only pieces of paper. By committing his act, he withdraws his obligation but remains responsibly faithful to it up to the *Instant Suprême*, after which he no longer can be held liable. In the message sent out, which is sometimes a cry for help, other times not, suicides proclaim two things: their loyalty to the contract (for they know absolutely that without a network of agreements there can be no social existence) and the triumph of the ego that only belongs to them, that ego which, to be sure, is only adopted in its totality as one's own possession as soon as one grasps that, while indeed everything that has been established intersubjectively as reality is valid, there is a way out of the order of things. Let us try to translate the message of suicides into everyday language. The action of each says: you others, as a part of the social network, were right against me, regardless of what you inflicted upon me; but look, I can withdraw myself from the validity of being right. And I am doing this without doing anything to you.

And by the way, he also says farewell. He says it was very nice. He sobs to himself (with or without glandular secretion, it's all the same): too bad that I have to go. He laments his fate, his misfortune. He's not a hero. He is even less an epistemologist. Regardless of how deep his disgust might be, how unconquerable his inclination to death, how triumphantly momentary his victorious ego might behave in his abdication of reality, how magnificent he might seem to himself in assuming his loneliness, now changing from a relative loneliness to an absolute one, how long the decision might have grown to maturity or with what sudden violence he might have taken hold of it, how high he might experience himself to have risen or how deep to have fallen: a suicide is a *human being*. He already belongs to the earth, but the earth still belongs to him—and it is beautiful. And the other, my God, it was, seen from the perspective of departure, not so frightening. Obeying reality, the suicide has made all the necessary arrangements to escape its principle. Reality could not be endured in its entirety, but since it had not only brought him the great *échecs* that were piled up within him but also the little hours of honor, maybe it wasn't quite so bad after all. A word sent in its direction, one that doesn't have to be written or even spoken, is the least one owes it. *Voilà, des fruits, des feuilles, des fleurs et des branches, et puis voici mon corps.* (Here are fruits, leaves, flowers, and boughs, and then here is my body.) I know, reality, how you will proceed with it. I have included everything in my calculations. And I came to the conclusion that I belonged to you and finally have to belong to myself. You, the other who was hell to me, but also bliss, won't mourn for me, at least not for long; but I am mourning for you and in you for myself. And with that, good night.

For those theoreticians of voluntary death who steadfastly and against all reason call it "self-murder," my message may be an act of aggression, an act of revenge or post-humous blackmail, who knows? —But I know. I know that the message, which is senseless, but without which I would not do what I am doing, is a hand stretched out in reconciliation. So, farewell. I belong finally to myself: I won't be able to harvest the fruits of my decision, but I'm satisfied with them, even in the *pain of separation*, which is great, especially when I consider that the world of a happy person is a different one from that of an unhappy person and that with death the world does not change, but stops.—This then is the meaning of the message, a message that can't arrive at its destination since it does not have one. The world is just as concrete as it is abstract: it is not experienced as the abstraction "world," but only concretely in images, other kinds of sense-impressions, even *ex*pressions, when I go so far as to take possession of them. To whom is the letter addressed? To a school friend who has been dead for a long time? To the Kathrin Mountains in the Salzkammergut in Upper Austria? To Gina? The address is the least clear when directed to those immediately closest. With them it's all settled. The mourning for them has been completed. A small legacy is officially validated and promised to the bereaved. Someone calls, and the echo that perhaps comes back from the mountains will no longer reach the one who called. That is known, even if the specialists in the name of God and the three devils are calmly taking the initial steps and developing points of access to construct hypotheses. Even that won't disturb me anymore. And if reality as language or talk comes to agree that I have in fact succumbed to a narcissistic crisis, even that will be fine with me.

The suicide is no longer an obstinate debater. He says

yes and amen: to himself and to the most extreme self-glorification of his ego and to the world, which condemns him out of hand with talk that is necessary to the preservation of the species. A feeling of dead calm? A head, running against four walls closing in upon each other, beating a frantic drumroll? One as well as the other, the metaphors only appear to exclude each other: in the place beyond, which doesn't exist, they, too, will cease to be.

V. The Road to the Open

A cell, perhaps four meters long, two meters wide. Any attempt to pace comes up against an impassable limit as soon as it's barely begun. How long is this to be endured? The "barrack room," in which a quantity of twenty prisoners have been quartered so that hardly any more space is de facto provided for each individual, more likely even less, seems by comparison to verge on freedom itself. Further desires for freedom will manifest themselves there. Access to the work area fenced in with barbed wire. A voice penetrates my ear, heard in times that have long since become historic. My comrade, packed together with me in a quarantine-barrack, said, "Tomorrow we will be free," and he actually meant by that: getting out of the half-darkness of the barracks into the limited day of the camp complex.

A man senses a constricting pressure in his chest, possibly because of the coronary insufficiency from which he suffers. He says to his physician, "Isn't there any remedy that can *free* me?" Again the idea I conceived in *On Aging* years ago, that every desire for freedom goes back to the physically conditioned and inalienable wish for the *freedom to breathe*. A sick person is not free to climb a mountain, at the summit of which he would be able to feel that he stands above the others and is thus superior to them. The prisoner is not free to buy a newspaper for himself at a newspaper stand. A poor man is not free to go to Rome or San Francisco. But the demand for freedom, actually reducible perhaps to the demand of the *physis* for oxygen, theoretically knows no limits both in its ramifications and in the process of its developments. And why am I not granted the freedom to own a yacht, to cruise the seas? To have empty space around me in which the noise from my neighbor's radio is lost? Why not the freedom to be lazy? Why not the freedom to throw away the burden of my body, which I know all too well? Every freedom for which I thirst is strictly conditioned by its correlative constraint. I feel myself restricted in my freedom when a red light at a street crossing orders me to stop. However, if one were to get rid of all the signaling systems in my city, it would be the congested cars of the others that would deny me the freedom to continue driving. The feeling of freedom that comes after its implied constraint has disappeared is always very short, and one immediately finds oneself in a hard-pressed situation again, from which it is necessary to break out. This insight into the necessity of the limits of my freedom is of little use to me. I know that wherever my aspirations take me, it is never my freedom, only resignation. I am not free to lift 150 pounds off the ground with one arm; my physical constitution won't allow it. That is necessity. I see into it and grasp it—that doesn't make the renunciation easier. Freedom is not an existential. Such may be the desire for freedom and along with it the gratification that occurs from time to time after breaking a constraint in an act of liberation; but it never lasts long.

What I am presenting here should not be misused to jump to the conclusion that political forms of freedom are only chimeras. They are not chimeras because whenever they are limited, the urgent wish to set them up is expressed. Habeas corpus, free speech, free elections: they don't mean much when I have them. Granting them is essential when they are of no advantage to me. The Chilean worker wants to be free to vote or to oppress the oppressor. The Czecho-slovakian writer suffocates in bondage when he is not al-lowed the possibility of publishing what he has written. The fact that, as soon as the one can vote and the other publish, new constraints get in the way of both is another matter. Freedom is not an unchangeable space to be conquered once and for all: it is a permanent process of new and ever new liberations. These liberations do not persist as consolations for being. But whenever they cannot be put into practice, existence is unbearable. And if freedom is not an existen-tial, acts of liberation, one after the other, are. They belong to the fundamental project of every individual and last throughout one's life. A child demands freedom from the compulsion of school. A youth would like to rip the tablets of the sexual commandments out of the ground. A man wants the freedom to go to the woman he chooses and away from the binding law of marriage. An old man cries gently for liberation from his own powerlessness. In the end ev-eryone makes the compromises that are necessary to have one's own demands for liberation accommodate themselves

to others who are also carrying out their process of liberation. In all cases the compromise is lame or stale. It's always
half a compromise; the contract is signed with reservations.
And is also broken. So that a new one, signed again with
reservatio mentalis, can be entered into.

As a product of the basic human condition, every act of
liberation changes both the past and the future. A new
project is conceived. This not only alters whatever has been
valid up to now, but also the past related to it. One man was
an architect and decided at a definite moment of his life to
become a writer. He liberated himself, as it were, from the
architect he was and in doing so liquidated not only his
architectural plans for the future but also his study of this
subject. Freedom, or liberation, as we are wont to say, negates a definite way of being. It is just as constructive as it is
destructive. As something human, it is clearly in all conditions more of a negation than an affirmation. And it no doubt
affirms a project whose realization is of course uncertain.
But above all it denies a condition alleged under compulsion. Thus a piece of wood in the hands that carve it no
longer remains itself. It becomes the negation of what was
only wood. And because liberation is destruction, it finds its
most extreme possible confirmation in voluntary death. That
doesn't hold true? Then liberation as denial would be just
denial and it would only be actual liberation with respect to
a project within a particular human existence and its constantly new possibilities? And death would be precisely, just
as Sartre said, no longer a part of my possibilities? And therefore I was right some time ago when I wrote the phrase
about the "fool's story of a voluntary death?" This remains
to be seen.

At this moment we are not yet at the crossroads where views have to differ. Let's just continue holding forth with the discourse on freedom, for the present. It is said that we should make a distinction between freedom *to* something and freedom *from* something: thus being free on the one hand to do something forbidden to us by a constraint and on the other being free from something that torments us or even just disturbs us. Actually they are both one. For when I say I would like to be nothing else but free *from* the pressure in my chest then I don't mean that I want to be set free in order to fade away in a condition of feeling no pressure. I want to throw the burden from my thorax in order to be able to move on like others. I want to be freed from the prohibition against free speech in order to be permitted to speak. From the burden of poverty in order to travel (or even just to eat).

Whether I am conscious of it as such or only as an inarticulate desire, the project has precedence; and every freedom *from* means a freedom *to*. I spoke at the beginning of a very old man, sick to death, who told me that his last days had come and during a moment when his condition deceptively seemed to have improved, he demanded his favorite food, brussels sprouts. That is, he did not want to be free from his agonizing stomach pains in order to be—or not only in order to be—free of them, but to be able to consume those brussels sprouts. Thus, we liberate ourselves permanently in order to be something or to do something that changes our existence and negates and makes nothing of what we presently do or allow. The *ex-sistere* is a negation of the fetters of our being and is carried out as long as we are here. "I would like to get up, doctor," a very sick person says. "May I leave the office earlier today?" asks an employee. "I want to write something," a writer thinks, "something that goes beyond what I've brought out so far, I want to be free *from* what I've done *to* do what I have in mind to do." And so, may one speak of the urge to be free *from* something—*to* nothing? No, as we have seen. Yes: *because there is voluntary death*; and it posits, rarely, as it may always be, the limit of thinking existentially and leads reflection to a new shore. At this moment the metaphor needs to be taken back: there are no shores. But voluntary death exists and removes us, delivers us from a state of being that has become a burden and from the *ex-sistere* that has become nothing but fear. Thus, it is clear that the question about the sense and nonsense of voluntary death has to be asked anew, at the risk of not being able to answer it. But if we ask the question without the hope of an answer, then we rise up in revolt against Wittgenstein's claim: "To an answer that does not exist, one cannot express the question as well."[1] Only, this statement is—Oh logical syntax of language!—not a declaration, but an imperative. It does not have to be—and cannot be—followed. The "questioning awe" of which Ernst Bloch speaks takes hold of us even when we know that it will not find any satisfaction or peace.

And so, as we see—I'm not going to say "clearly," but with enough lack of clarity that from now on we won't be able to look away from it—, voluntary death, which promises freedom *from* something, but without also being freedom *to* something, as logic requires, is, more than just affirmation of dignity and humanity, directed against the blind reign of nature. It is liberty in the most extreme and final form that we can attain. *"L'histoire d'une vie, quelle qu'elle soit, est l'histoire d'un échec"* (The story of a life, whatever it might be, is the story of an *échec*), writes Sartre. This *échec* is for him the petrified being that every kind of existing becomes: the hunt for the freedom of the *ex-sistere*, which wants to wrest itself from being and is again and again overtaken by it, finds its end in death. *"C'est la mort qui change une vie en destin,"* (It is death that changes a life into a destiny) says André Malraux, and our destiny, because it still ends in death, our negation, is an unhappy one. The hunt is given up; without having caught anything, the hunter heads for the inexpressible. And shouldn't it be considered freedom to make one's own decision to break off the chase? In the knowledge that disgust with being is fundamentally the same as that with the *ex-sistere*, shouldn't voluntary death be, in the double sense of the word, my *last* freedom? Then, too, even logic, as the logic of life, has constantly had to capitulate, and propositions disposed of as false by positivistic philosophy have survived: consolation preserved for the disconsolate. Heine: "Sleep is good, death is better—of course / The best would be never to have been born."[2] Here we have one of those utterances, quickly shooed away as "empty formulae," which have had a continued existence up to now and which will go on existing, well beyond the lifetime of the philosophy of positivism. It is certainly clear: something that is best could only be best if it is experienced and "the unborn," which logically cannot be addressed as such, never experiences anything bad, good, or best. But of more consequence is the fact that many individuals carry Heine's wish within, know it to be more deeply sunken in, and more securely innate to, existence than any arbitrary religious phantasm or a metaphysically conceived fiction, which always finds it easy, with its hypotheses of goodwill, to dissolve primal contradictions. It is easy for thoughts to coexist. But the desire to be no more and not to exist is not a "thought" in the usual meaning of the word, and is therefore difficult. For those who consider voluntary death know exactly that they do not resolve the contradiction. Instead, it lives until the rupture, until the discontinuity that is the end of all continuities. The phenomenal facts have little to do with logic. Life—understood here as "being" as much as *ex-sistere*—is a burden. The day about to begin is an oppressive weight. Our own body is a weight, a body that certainly carries us but one that we also have to carry—and I have never understood how fat people can endure with themselves. Work is a burden, leisure is burdensome. The apartment with its furniture is ponderous. Street noises and the noises of human voices have to be endured, even borne—how clever everyday language is. The erect penis is heavy, even heavier the hanging one. Even the most tender breast has to be dragged along. Four walls are also constantly closing in on us. They will crush us to pieces and will be a burden. How does one say it? My heart is heavy, *j'ai le coeur lourd*. Are psychological motivations still required? Certainly. But they are always only the masks behind which the primal facts of existence are hidden. It was then that Otto Weininger noticed the burdensome burden, unbearable and unendurable in the fact that in his insane world, peopled by disgraceful women and more disgraceful Jews, it was not good to live. It was then that Lt. Gustl could not *bear* the idea that he would have to exchange the Kaiser's uniform for wretched civilian clothes. At that point a life that denied her the love of her radio idol was too hard for the servant girl.

We need to consider if what I am presenting is only valid for those who have already developed for themselves a constitution that is suicidal. For haven't I said myself that life is *world*? In skiing, a winter wind that is icy and biting but victoriously overpowered. In jumping, air as light as wings. In taking hold of something, a body that one loves, meat to be devoured, something hostile that one kills, loved one, meat, and opponent. A question, not answered, but almost fearfully posed: don't the suicidal know better? And doesn't what they know have to be binding for everyone? Because wind, loved one's body, meat, and enemy, become things in the very act of being seized, and I with them. So what remains is burden and corpse. Disgust with life arises, as well as disgust with what remains, even when it is a tender memory. And one flings burdens from oneself, both in freedom and to liberate oneself. But because, as we saw, the freedom that follows the liberation from the weight of being and existing is not experienced and the act of voluntary death is therefore senseless (certainly not in the twilight of carrying it out, but in looking toward the goal it strives for), and because after the death I've chosen for myself I will be neither free nor unfree, because I won't even be (and the word "be" is already too much)—for what reason are such inexpressibly difficult obstacles overcome and such violent demands on the instinct suppressed? Yes, for what reason? For no reason, unless it is to submit to what I have named the inclination toward death. But even such a submission is only a deliverance as long as I am living. —Here I think we have finally come to the crux of our discourse: voluntary death as a pure and most extreme negation that no longer conceals anything positive in itself so that in its presence all dialectics, just as much as all progressive logic, are frustrated and may in fact be "senseless."

To catch my breath I'm going to stop at the logic of life and try to evade its contradictions; which doesn't mean that I am going to submit myself completely to its law. Once again at home in it, in that which alone can be expressed in language *as* logic without pretext of metaphor, I'm going to make an attempt with the following to connect these strands of thought. Even if voluntary death, understood this way, is senseless, that is not the case with the *decision* to kill oneself. This decision, as we know, aiming at death but not subservient to the anti-logic of death, is not only made in freedom but also brings real freedom to us. I am coming back to what I have called the "*Abiturient*-situation." A student, who in view of the apparently insurmountable difficulties of the courses he is taking has stopped studying and is familiar with the idea that he will flunk, is free of the unbearable pressure of thinking about the exam. Translate this passage of Horace. Solve this equation. Interpret the line by Hölderlin. But my dear master, I'm not thinking about that at all! I don't care at all about Horace and Hölderlin and all equations put together. What do you want from me? I will flunk: and what else? Perhaps I will shoot myself in the morning frost like Heinrich Lindner. Perhaps I will follow the lucrative career of a pimp—and over the years you will still be standing before me, just a poor wretch in a funny and poorly cut suit. An aging actor, facing the prospect of a comeback in a new staging of *Macbeth*, a role he does not feel up to because of the modern performance code, says, "Thanks. I won't come back. I'd rather stay where I am. And shit on your production."[3] An official, seeing his last chance to become the manager of his department disappear, thinks to himself, "Good, I'm going to get out of here right away, someone will still take me on somewhere else, the hierarchy is ridiculous, tomorrow it won't concern me anymore." It is no different with the decision to kill oneself, even if it doesn't promise any accommodation. At the moment when a human being says to himself he can throw away his life, he is already becoming free, even if it is in a monstrous way. The experience of freedom is overwhelming. For now nothing is valid anymore. The burden? It only has to be carried for a few more yards; throwing it away is anticipated in an ecstasy that stands high above every other kind of intoxication. The question whether this is escape, escape and evasion, remains open. The movement of escape goes *from* something *to* something: there, behind me, the prison with its cells, before me the freedom of the night in the forest or under a bridge. But a potential suicide doesn't believe in finding shelter anywhere, even though one may say a hundred times as a habit of speaking that one is escaping from confinement into open space, from struggle into peace. Each knows that nothing changes, but that everything ceases. A precondition of one's decision as an act of liberation is still that one is *serious* about it. There are many who will say, "If everything goes wrong, I can always kill myself." After that, everything does go wrong and they continue to live wrong, yet a little poorer, sadder, older, sicker, lonelier, and their proud resolution soon becomes just a distant memory; a landscape, once glimpsed in a vision, whose gentle meadows were never trodden. Authentic potential suicides don't make it so easy on themselves. The act of dying, perhaps painfully, dragging on without vouchsafing the possibility that one is acting freely, can forestall one. Then one thinks, "Why haven't I?" Now advancing only with a limp, perhaps it is because one has to recognize that one has missed the right moment; one's concern is getting to be one's shame about one's own failure. The *burning shame*. The moment of decision that lifted one up still remains irrevocable: Once I was living like the gods and now nothing more is needed. Those outside are free to think what they want. One of them has always let it be known that he'd rather be dead than a slave,[4] would rather remove himself from the world in dignity, humanity, and liberty than suffer the humiliation of his loss of significance. And look, there he is, still living. A big talker. One who lost his life without gaining death. People like us have fended for themselves by taking blows and displacing them when it was not all too dangerous. People like us are not misdeveloped individuals and poor fools.—

I'm going to put everything in order. And especially this: That disgust with being and an inclination toward death, in their totally oppressive and *depressive* forms, are only felt by a negligibly slight number of human beings. All the others don't need to let bitter talk embitter their adherence to being and existence, which is just as much an illusion as it is biologically prescribed. They never lived like gods and never needed to. They gave their affirmation and negation in a state of equilibrium that their respective others, whoever they were, packaged as "world" for them, and when it did not balance, they faked the counterbalance with the best social and biological conscience. In the twinkling of an eye humiliation and *échec* became something for them to overcome: it is sometimes nothing more than the pure result of time. Then the poor devil says to himself: "So, I've put all this behind me. And because of that, haven't I been brave and haven't I deserved every honor?" He accepts human existence with all its misery. The passage of time and letting it pass, each helps him. And it's drawing to an end. Insofar as he can still take thought—for the final days, beating like a hammer, make his head numb—he thinks he's fulfilled his duty. Here he cannot be disputed: how would that even be possible? For those who are true to the duties of life, who represent the human being plain and simple, they are certainly constituted in this characteristic by biology and society. Their concern, the immensely majoritarian and therefore normal concern, is stolen from them first by the death they challenge, in fear and trembling, both of which may also be called bravery. A potential suicide cuts a small figure in front of them, like a body of troops that is cut off from the main body and overtaken by the more powerful opposing army, just as it was with the French soldiers who were cut off for such a long time in Sartre's novel *Iron in the Soul*. Only a few, among them Mathieu Delarue, kept shooting from the church tower at the advancing enemy, up to the last bullet. Heroes? Don't make me laugh! Only a few who'd gone astray, for whom dignity, humanity, and liberty stood higher than life in the stalag and what was yet to come afterwards. Those who entered the prison camp without their weapons were right: many of them are still living today. Those who shot from the church tower, however, were not on that account wrong. They and the others chose what was theirs and no one can be the judge of either. That society has already passed judgment on the marksmen in the church is a fact. I am not casting aspersions on the overpowering facticity of this judgment when I put my word in for those who fought the losing battle up in the tower. And because we have considered them to be suicidal, the question has to concern us again and from another angle whether someone who gives himself to death is really *free*.

Now we're no longer dealing with the logical problem of whether freedom from something (the burden of being) is still freedom if it doesn't immediately set us free to do something. To put it plainly, we are standing before the question mark that is still behind the concept of the *freedom of the will*. Just about everything has been said about it so that it seems like a childish presumption when I venture into an area where the keenest minds have seriously injured themselves on the invisible reefs in the fog of every kind of philosophizing. What I want to say here, in order to bring this talk to a partially good end, is hardly new and certainly not revolutionary, but perhaps it will still help us to go one step further on our way. If I am seeing things correctly, we have to take ourselves into a realm that lies beyond determinism and indeterminism. We will therefore be spared the misunderstanding of basing the freedom of the will on the knowledge of modern physics, which, even though it has overthrown mechanical determinism, is still of no use to us here because we're not concerned with the "behavior" of elemental particles (they don't behave at all and to use the verb in this context is nonsense!), but with the decisions of human beings. They are, these incidents of decision, certainly not "free" insofar as freedom is translated by lack of causality.

Those who make the decision to extinguish their existence are like the majority who decide in the same situation to live on: they are subject to a multi-causality that is almost infinite. Heredity, the influence of the environment, imponderable specific details of their situation, even circumstances of intellectual history, "accidents" as well as "necessities," both causally (or even just statistically) and mechanically defined (which comes to the same thing), lead potential suicides to the point at which the almost infinitely numerous causal series intersect in such a way that each bleeds to death from them. It is just that these particular causal series constitute their ego and are felt by them as their ego. A drug addict says to himself that he is unfortunately addicted and therefore not free. But every decision to take drugs is lived as an act of will precisely *because* counterdeterminates stand as hindrances in the way of the enjoyment of the product. In the space of the *vécu* human beings are with their ego and, as their ego, are free—which means here: they experience themselves as free and act, must act, as if they were free. Our existence teaches us this and all scholarly learning comes out empty because it is empty. We could not exist another hour if we were to wait for these causal series to drag us somewhere. We are conditioned: but we experience ourselves as free. To view lived existence in the rigorous sense of the natural sciences as "causally defined" would be just as senseless, no, much more senseless and destructive of life, as to believe in a transcendental freedom of the will that is empty of perception and thus situated beyond every possibility of experience. Reservations and "reasonable compromises" are also indispensable to such considerations. It is true that the transcendental freedom of the will is for us nothing but a word, born from words. Likewise it is still right to say that the skeins of causality in their totality and their inextricable entanglement form our ego, the cogito that not only thinks but also acts and in its thinking and acting is experienced as free. It must be conceded that the experienced and lived freedom of the will has *degrees* that at any time expand or limit the personal experience of free action (in ten minutes I will call again; tomorrow I am driving to Bordeaux; in the next few months I have to finish my new book). Sartre gives the example of the prisoner: he is not free, but he is free to choose whether he wants to try to break out of the prison or not. "It isn't what has been made of a human being that counts but what one makes of what one was made for." Things that are insurmountably and indelibly true and things that are badly exaggerated by thinking in principles are mingled here and it is not easy to unmix them. For the prisoner hampered by an injured foot the decision to break out will be more difficult than for the healthy prisoner, and maybe even impossible. I will call again in ten minutes—as long as my boss isn't on the phone; I can't interrupt his call. Tomorrow I am driving to Bordeaux, "if nothing intervenes at the last minute," as a cautious speaker would say. "In the next few months I must and will finish my book," says the old writer and thinks, "If I don't die first, with a fragment left on my desk." A drunk is not free to drive a car as he would normally; his reactions have been made slower. —And I'm already in danger of going astray and entering a realm that I have forbidden myself for reasons of my incompetence: the broad land of psychology. Therefore I'm going to stop. I only want to repeat that I am free, because my ego is still absorbing the limitations of its selfhood; that there are, however, degrees of this state of being free, and I am not free in the same way today as I will be tomorrow or yesterday as I was the day before. Still, the question occupying us, whether and in what measure voluntary death is actually a free death, can be discussed without us having to pursue psychology in the narrow, entirely special sense of a branch of science.—Neither it nor, by the way, sociology.

In those moments when we take just a fleeting glance at the suicidological literature, it becomes convincingly clear that there is only a very small quantity of "pre-suicidal" situations that would not be mastered by an overwhelming majority—or to put it better: from which the majority would not find a way back into life. No doubt there are psychologists and psychiatrists ready to reproach us by demonstrating that this is surely an irrefutable proof of the lack of freedom in what is to them this unacceptable act of voluntary death; that precisely at this point it becomes totally clear that the will of suicides and potential suicides is no longer free: if they weren't "disturbed people" who were in a situation they had been forced into because they were no longer fully in possession of their ego, they would act like the majority of all human beings. We need to ask whether such an objection does not result from a logical error. Here, the premise that the right thing to do is always to go on living, no matter how, seems to be turning itself into the conclusion. At the moment when I fail to insert majoritarian behavior as an absolute *value* that conditions all considerations, the premise and the ostensible conclusion fall away. X has killed himself in a situation in which Y, Z, and all letters of the alphabet and all conceivable symbols live on. Is X, the outsider, more powerless? Does X lack a better hold of his willpower? Or is precisely *his* will free as well as strong?

I shall take care not to decide. But I will also keep myself from being influenced by the case histories from which it clearly follows that X, the suicide, has always been quite different from the others. Difficulties with parents. An education that went wrong. Early delinquency in one case, authenticated neurotic symptoms in another. What does that mean to me? In the best of cases I can make the almost amusing argument that similar dispositions and constellations did not obstruct the way into life of others, thus concluding that suicides are free in making their decision. Free. And alone. But not completely; otherwise, as we had to recognize, they would not send out a message with their act. But alone in actually going through with the plan they've decided to carry out. In that no one has a companion: double suicides, as they're called, are rare, and even in those rare cases each is alone, both the one urging to the act as well as the one urged. And each one is free, corresponding to the degree of his or her freedom in its totality. If anywhere at all, then Sartre's sentence is valid here: "Actually, *we* are freedom that chooses; but we don't choose to be free." No one can experience the damnation to freedom more intensively than the suicide. For here one strides in freedom and with it to the end of every freedom, an end that in its irreversibility is no longer even a compulsion from which one can plan to break out.

It could appear that here only freedom of thought is contemplated. Sire, give freedom of thought . . ., etc.[5] Most people get nothing out of it because the issue is not to think freely but to act freely. Otherwise, we find ourselves in the thickets of "inwardness," the cheap freedom of the Christian man who talks with his God but is respectfully silent before his prince until the latter says, "Speak, fellow." It would certainly seem that we are dealing with freedom of thought here in two ways: first, in the way the full freedom in the decision to take one's life is known, a decision one makes in a state of rupture and discontinuity and decidedly maintains up to the moment "before the leap"; and second, in the way that freedom as a broad land, even as the open—as when one says, "Let's go out in the open a bit"—is never experienced. But because, on the other hand, as presented and thought through logically, a resolution to kill oneself only acquires the value of freedom or liberation through the fact that each potential suicide is serious about what he or she is doing, the decision *pro suicido* extends well beyond freedom of thought. Preparations are made (during a space of time: longer, shorter, or even just a few seconds, it can be right before it happens); they are therefore not thought, but *done*, as is always the case when thinking has become a form of action and lost its character of play. The freedom to choose voluntary death is not the suspect freedom of the Christian man. I am not concerned with God in the process of preparation, but with a weapon, a rope, with grayish-green waters in which my eye gets lost, or with the asphalt upon which I stare from the seventeenth story. The seriousness of the resolution and the determination that follows are fatal: and the liberation will be fatal, and the freedom will disappear with the violent escape from constriction. Thus voluntary death is a breath-giving *road to the open*, but not this open itself. Which does not destroy the dreamlike beauty of this road, even if it is overgrown with the thorns of the pain of separation.

When I wrote the title at the head of this chapter, taking it from Arthur Schnitzler's great novel and making it my own, I knew well that it would lead again to a contradiction. The road to the open is a road if and only if I follow it seriously, but in this case it leads nowhere. If I wander forward on the other hand, not in bitter determination but promenade on it just for a few hours, as if walking in the spring wind through bare avenues, then it is no way at all. Then the decision is no decision and the liberation is a farce. This was clear to me. What I wasn't thinking about was the novel itself which, by using its title, I quoted as a symbol. This book, like all the literary productions of Schnitzler, has "a most unhappy end." All its figures strive toward the road to the open. But then they die like Anna Rosner or fall into dutiful subordination like the writer Heinrich Bermann. Schnitzler, appraised and condemned as a coquettish five-dollar bon vivant of the world of literature, one who "precociously and tenderly and sadly" plays his games, is in truth the great connoisseur of senseless living and dying, a friend of death, as intimate with it as was Thomas Mann, one who knew about the kind of love that is pregnant with death as deeply as Marcel Proust, one who finally knew of voluntary death, which in a ghostly way again and again emerges in his works, not only in *Lt. Gustl*, but also in the terrifying piece *Sterben* (Dying), in the novella *Spiel im Morgengrauen* (Gambling at daybreak), in the play *Das Märchen* (The fairy tale). He knew that for the potential suicide as well as for anyone who in resignation or a state of idle oblivion continues to play a game without rules, the road to the open only leads again and again into one wilderness or another: it may be death or the resignation of one who no longer believes in anything and who no longer esteems himself.[6]

I hope I've been forgiven this deviation. But I need to add immediately that it really wasn't one. I was anxious to call attention to the extent to which we are exposed to absurdity. By that I don't mean the kind evoked by Albert Camus in an arbitrary context in his peculiarly willful way. *L'absurde* is really both more everyday and more terrifying than the myth of Sisyphus. Each of us experiences the absurd, but only a few take the experience to themselves and take it thinking and acting to the end, "think-acting" I would like to write if the word didn't sound so tortured. *On s'arrange* (One manages): this formula, one of the most common in colloquial French, concisely mirrors the facts. Proust's narrator, when Albertine left him, suffered beyond words; finally he managed the facts of his reality so well that when he heard of her death, Albertine was not even worth a tear. The total absurdity of life, which itself constantly consumes itself, is mediated to us by contemporary history: "It passes by, afterwards it made no difference," said Karl Kraus in his famous and infamous poem at the outbreak of the Third Reich.[7] Hitler. He was to us, to those he most of all singled out to take aim at—how can I say it?—whom he would have roasted over a small fire, he was radical evil plain and simple. What is he today? To the youngest something historical like Nero, not exactly invoking sympathy, but not worth much further talk. To the older a scoundrel among others; since then, all too many political crimes have become known. To those who were themselves directly affected and battered? Let's be honest: with time and through time the absurd self-consuming nature of life has already blurred Hitler's abominable shape even for them. I don't think much anymore of that enemy of the human race; I have to be challenged to be agitated. History makes sense of the senseless, inasmuch as one wants to take the trouble to make sense, but something one will avoid once the senselessness is known. Theodor Lessing[8] was not so querulously obstructive as he is said to be and Hegel probably not as great as the virtual terrorism of daily opinion hammers into us. Knowledge of the absurdity of life, which can also be an *échec* when a champion of vitality swaggers and shows off in his laurels, leads directly to the thought of voluntary death; it isn't necessary to have a specific conflict situation established first. But if this knowledge is added to our absurd fundamental condition, half-and-half lived, half-and-half thrust from consciousness, it makes this condition clear in a frightening way. At that point the burden that we have to carry around becomes unbearable and existence confronts us as an examination that is impossible to pass. And so we try to find the road to the open, even those of us who know that it's a wild goose chase or, in a contemporary metaphor, one of those streets that is just as easy to navigate as all others but that is marked with traffic signs with red crossbeams as a dead end by the traffic authorities. I often travel this street in order to try the matter out: it's always right. Villas become sparse left and right. Then at the end, a scanty little woods or farmstead that prohibits any kind of continued journey. The way back. The maneuver to turn around. And constantly the pressing wish simply to drive on, precisely in that direction where there is no further driving on, on into the woods and over hedge and ditch as if the car were a tank, or against the wall of the house as if I were steering a bulldozer. The drive back to the unopen has something annihilating about it, even though it also has—and one has to persist in this—a shamefully comforting aspect. The boulevards stretch out in their stately manner—who would have thought so beforehand, while being tempted to drive car and woods and the wall of the villa to ruin? The little streets accept the driver, they act as if they knew nothing of the frightening longing he felt a short time ago. They act—what nonsense! They don't do anything. They're simply small traffic arteries, indifferent, not even indifferent, just opaque, like the narrowing coronary vessels, which, even for the sick, do not "prepare" pains (they neither do nor let anything), but as a part of the enemy world they just cause them; thus one elementary particle causes motion of another, without love, without hate. The driver of the car turns toward home. There everything is also alien and hostile: the book that he doesn't like to read, the typewriter whose hammering becomes murderous over time. And the wish for the road to the open becomes more urgent. Not that the knowledge was deceiving, as one might expect. It always conveys in a well-shaped and a logically and syntactically unobjectionable language, or even only in a drearily preconscious and partial clarity, that here the open is an empty thing. No Garden of Eden beckons with its resplendent fruit, no repose in the moss under the generous shadows of a tree, nothing is there except that cold and stony lunar landscape familiar to us since the first astronauts reached the satellite—and not even that.

The open is not anything open, but the road is the road

to the open, nevertheless. One enters upon it in order to end the torment and, in moving forward, sacrifices even the moments of elevation, never without the mourning of farewell, always in the feeling of throwing away a burden that became too heavy. Let what is coming be the business of the others. In the future they can make of me what they want, in forgetting and remembering, this is to be considered in advance, for even in that there is something like a lack of freedom. I was this and that. A writer is dragged for a while through literary history until people feel sorry for him. Thus Theodor Körner was made a great writer and thus he was disposed of; no one, except a few rare German scholars who are becoming even rarer, reads Körner's play *Zriny* any more. Other names were erased from the board more quickly: Theodor Kramer, Ernst Waldinger, and that other one, left behind, who ruined both of them with his indifferent forgetting.[9] Good old cabinetmakers and glovemakers don't have any surviving others except a few family members. They say, "What a good man he was and he liked to eat cabbage." That lasts for a little while, then even they say nothing more and even the cabbage-eater is forgotten. The name of someone held in cherished memory is eradicated from the gravestone because so much rain has fallen. In the most optimal situation a dead person would become a mummy and the subject of art or history. Nefertiti's head is considered beautiful. What she was has become the gossip of historians. Wallenstein said he was thinking of having a long sleep, and Golo Mann probably has him say even more.[10] Nothing brings up the world of the generalissimo again, a world that was his and *only* his. This means that with my road to the open I deliver myself over to the others, even further beyond recall than ever before in life when my project can certainly fail and actually does fail in most cases, *always* fails from the point of view of death, and is now not even visible any more. Hölderlin could not protest against Norbert von Hellingrath and is silent with respect to Pierre Bertaux.[11] *"La mort est un fait contingent,"* (Death is a contingency) says Sartre. Death certainly. But how does it stand with the special case of voluntary death? Here I think I can tear myself away from the other. As a free death in the sphere of my experience it is not a contingency, contrary to a so-called natural death. It is a project, a free one on the one hand. But because on the other hand I do not attain the open with it, it becomes in its final effect a new contingency and is therefore something totally mistaken—just as much as that which is only true with respect to one's own life's lie. It delivers me to the other insofar as the latter can now proceed with my terminated life according to whatever seems to be good or bad. But the other lifts me up beyond myself and destroys my delusions—with me.

A life's lie. Which one of us could step forward with the reckless assurance of having lived, not a lie, but one's own innate authenticity? None of us. Because the latter, which constantly constructs itself just to be itself, destroys itself permanently. The more zealously one pursues it, the more quickly it disappears in the mist. One can reconstruct one's life and follow its traces. What I experienced in 1919—my entry into elementary school, the immediate results of the collapse of a proud empire—became false in the light of 1930, became true in the perspective of 1940, and is once again a lie when I direct my eyes to it today. Was I already deceiving myself at the moment of my experience and am I de-

ceiving myself now at this hour? Am I making my yesterday just as much an untruth as my present and is perhaps
what has passed only wrong as a consequence of the light
of the lie I see it in today? Epistemologically the proof can
easily be furnished that the concept of truth (coincident here
with authenticity) cannot be legitimized. The certainty of a
false and dishonest life, of lying to the world and to oneself,
exists for everyone who reawakens in memory what is over
and done with in one's life—even without undertaking an
ingenious, theoretically supported self-analysis.

So much comes up, once the resolution to suicide becomes the final design of a human being. Tenderness for
oneself and disgust with life, blissful memories and the calamity of knowing about the lies of one's life enter into a
union that cannot be disentangled. Someone asks himself
why the girl from the dark resort park who smelled like
cheap soap and had a ridiculous name was built up by him
to be a *femme*, even a *femme fatale*, when she was already
fatal enough in a quite different sense. How did it come
about that another who in God's name had a Bohemian
snub nose, wore badly fitting clothes she'd made herself,
and was a poor slut in every respect, was imagined by him
to be the archetype of a spoiled feminine inscrutability? How
was it then possible that he, Macbeth in front of a public of
unsuspecting small-town people, became intoxicated with
childish applause? So many little lies adding up to a big one.
The examples reflect the silliness of everyday life: each one
wants to find for oneself other lies, somewhat more dignified.
That one has lived in a lie each will eventually grasp as
well, just as Sartre, when he said of his early works that,
while he was writing them, he had been *complètement mys-*

tifié (completely mystified). His book *The Words* is above all an attempt to cancel out the mystification of his own childhood: and it is, in all its literary splendor, another, a new mystification. The fact is that we only fully arrive at ourselves in a freely chosen death. It, and only it, is *"la minute de la verité* (the moment of truth). I think, therefore I am: the sense of this sentence can be doubted; no less a person than Wittgenstein did so. I die, therefore I will no longer be: that is unassailable; it is the rock of our subjective truth that becomes objective when we are dashed to pieces on impact.

Further argument that voluntary death in its contradictory nature is the only road to the open that stands available to us: *It is absurd but not foolish because it is clear that its absurdity does not increase the absurdity of life but decreases it.* The least that we may rightly concede to it is the taking back of all our life's lies that we endured and are able to endure only by virtue of just those lies. Sometimes I think that suicide must be less absurd than all those deaths that are thought of as an arcade, a passageway through to the absolute, as represented in certain pre-Columbian sculptures with little gates (actually only long slitted openings)—behind them stands nothing more. Passageways from nothing to nothing. Aesthetic game-playing, clearly yielding to an intense desire. There is no further thought, expressible in language, that can correspond to such a desire, and if I continue to forge the chain of these thoughts, I must recognize that the "absolute" is only a word. No imaginable reality corresponds to it, only one of unreal and unrealizable needs. There is really nothing to write home about. One says he longs for something but doesn't know what except that he longs to get away from something that, whatever it is, everyone clearly experiences as an affliction. Another speaks to us of his being drawn to God, that after death he will come close to Him. Asked about the distinct features of this God, he declines to provide any information, like a defendant who in response to an examining magistrate invokes his right to say nothing that could incriminate him and his case. But in doing that he is already incriminating himself: the judge takes note of his refusal as if it were a self-accusation. The concept of God, without a visual image and therefore empty, is no better than the absolute, and no one can play the trump with the Lord as the guarantor of the good sense of the utterance. To say in opposition that life as living-toward-death is absurd, arousing disgust in the opacity of its lies; that the inclination toward death is the only fitting posture for the burden of being; that the God of the other is imaginable only as a demiurge; and that voluntary death as a decision and an act, if not as a result as well, is an answer to all unsolvable questions that may be asked even without hope of an answer—to say such things is to put oneself in a better position than the man of God and of the absolute. The latter waits in submission until the reaper comes in any one of the many quite abominable and unreasonable shapes in which it is his pleasure to embody himself. A quick cardiac death is the most obliging. But what about a softening of the brain, at the end of which stands the paralysis of the respiratory center? What about cancer, the metastases of which make life materialize as a "stimulating proliferation of being" and make it felt in dreadful pain? What about when the kidneys go on strike and only strike-breaking instruments can get them back to work, leaving a breathing cadaver that lies in a hospital bed and rasps? I know that what Schopenhauer called the *will* (and he was no fool in using this term, even if it is conceptually overstrained to the point of exhaustion) and the instinct to preserve the ego and the species that makes us all live and endure, even to struggle to the end in a most unequal battle, already lost from the start, is so powerful that, though it cannot offset the absurdity of human existence, it probably can suppress it. I know that this will commands our respect. To obey it is to help nature realize itself and to be an executor of the most superior laws of being. But it would seem to be insane, even criminal, to exhort people to take the road to the open. "One still has to live," it is said, and "One wants to live" is the fact in front of us. But not everyone has to be "one." Those who raise an objection against the law in the name of humanity, dignity, and liberty, who within the absurd total system carry out *absurde résistance*, those are the ones we want to celebrate, not as heroes—that would be just as ridiculous as veteran ceremonies—but to let their despised and reviled action be valid. It should be what the suicide wants it to be: a road—and we can deny ourselves the gratuitous mockery that it's not a road to the open. With the words of Villon and Brecht that were meant for the poor, suicides approach us: "You brothers of humanity, you who will live after us / Don't let your hearts harden against us. . ."[12] But the request won't be granted. Hearts are hardening in a most unbrotherly way; they have to, otherwise their mechanism would break to pieces. Those who take the road to the open do well to include this, too, in their calculations. It will be as if they had never been or as if they had been *in a different way*: an equation that comes out to zero.

Nothing more remains to be said. Or I would have to begin again with the situation "before the leap." And everything would repeat, without an end, like a canon, a song that no one completely sings to the end. From here no path of thinking goes onward. The circle is closed. If we look closely at it, we begin to brood about it; we don't find its beginning any more than its end. Only with this metaphor do our meditations on voluntary death arrive at their conclusion: but it can no more be lived through than death itself. What can be experienced is only the absurdity of life and death and—when voluntary death is chosen—an absurd intoxication of freedom. The value of this experience is not slight. For just as a bolt of lightning thrills us, the knowledge thrills us, when things have gone far enough, that the whole of everything was in essence the untrue.[13] But that is knowledge that doesn't count for anything in life. For even potential suicides, when they approach the threshold of the leap, must show that they are up to the presumptions of life, otherwise they would not find their road to the open and would be like the concentration camp inmate who doesn't dare to run against the electrified fence, would still like to gulp down his evening soup and then the hot acorn soup in the morning and again a turnip soup at noon, and on and on. Still: a requirement of life is here— and not only here—the demand to escape a life lacking in dignity, humanity, and freedom. And so death becomes life, just as from the moment of birth life is already a process of dying. And now negation all at once becomes something positive, even if good for nothing. Logic and dialectic fail in tragicomic agreement. What counts is the option of the subject. But the survivors are right: for what are dignity, humanity, and freedom in preference to smiling, breathing, and striding? What is value against right and being correct? Dignity in opposition to the provision of every form of being dignified? And humanity against a human being as a living, smiling, breathing, striding creature?

Things don't go well with potential suicides and haven't turned out the best for suicides. We ought not to deny them respect for what they have done and left undone, we ought not to deny them concern, especially since we ourselves do not cut such a splendid figure. We look lamentable, anyone can see that. And so, subdued and in an orderly manner, with lowered heads, we want to offer a lament for those who departed from us in freedom.

NOTES

TRANSLATOR'S INTRODUCTION

1. Erika Tunner, "Die 'ambiguité' des Alterns," in *Jean Améry [Hans Maier]*, ed. Stephan Steiner (Basel and Frankfurt am Main: Stroemfeld/ Nexus, 1996), 251.

2. *On Suicide* was first published by Ernst Klett Verlag in Stuttgart in 1976 as *Hand an sich legen. Diskurs über den Freitod* (To lay hands on oneself: A discourse on voluntary death). *Lefeu* (1974) and *Charles Bovary, Landarzt* (1978) were also published by Klett. *On Aging: Revolt and Resignation* appeared with the same publisher under the title *Über das Altern. Revolte und Resignation* in 1968 and in my translation with Indiana University Press in 1994.

3. Quoted in *Text und Kritik 99: Jean Améry* (July 1988), 67.

4. J. P. Stern, *Lichtenberg: A Doctrine of Scattered Occasions* (Bloomington: Indiana University Press, 1959), 317 (aphorism J1186 in Lichtenberg's *Schriften und Briefe*, vol. I: *Sudelbücher I*, ed. Wolfgang Promies, 3rd ed. [München: C. Hanser, 1980], 820).

5. Jean Améry, *"Hand an sich legen—Exposé,"* in: *Hermannstraße 14, Halbjahrschrift für Literatur. Sonderheft Jean Améry* (Stuttgart: Klett-Cotta, 1978), 15.

6. Jean Améry, *Unmeisterlich Wanderjahre* (Wanderings without mastery) (Stuttgart: E. Klett, 1971), 41.

7. Jean Améry, *Cinéma. Arbeiten zum Film* (Stuttgart: Klett-Cotta, 1994), 71, 84f.

8. Lothar Baier, "'Die zarte Haltung': Die Kritik des schreibenden Lesers Jean Améry," in: *Jean Améry [Hans Meier]*, ed. Stephan Steiner (Basel and Frankfurt am Main: Stroemfeld/Nexus, 1996), 217–33; and Jean Améry, "Bergwanderung," in: Jean Améry, *Der integrale Humanismus*, ed. Helmut Heißenbüttel (Stuttgart: Klett-Cotta, 1985), 110–33.

9. Jean Améry, "Atemnot," in *Der integrale Humanismus*, ed. Helmut Heißenbüttel, 267–73.

10. Améry, "Begegnungen mit Elias Canetti," in *Der integrale Humanismus*, ed. Helmut Heißenbüttel, 219, 221.

11. See Dagmar Lorenz, *Scheitern als Ereignis: Der Autor Jean Améry im Kontext europäischen Kulturkritik* (Frankfurt am Main: P. Lang, 1991), 46– 59. For a perceptive discussion of Améry's suicide, see Susan Neiman,

"Jean Améry Takes His Life," in: *Yale Companion to Jewish Writing and Thought in German Culture, 1096–1966*, ed. Sander L. Gilman and Jack Zipes (New Haven: Yale University Press, 1997), 775–82.

12. Susan Neiman singles out this passage for its summation of Améry's view of what is important in human life (ibid., 782): "Nowhere does Améry's apparently endless sympathy for two sides of a contradiction achieve more startling expression than in the final page of his treatise on suicide. . . . This coda follows a stunning tribute to the ideas of dignity, humanity, and freedom—one that goes so far as to defend the act of suicide as a means that may be chosen to protect them."

PREFACE

1. As in *On Aging*, Améry is much influenced by Jean-Paul Sartre (1905–1980), especially *L'être et le néant*, first published in Paris (Gallimard) in 1943.It was published in English as *Being and Nothingness* in 1956 by Philosophical Library (New York).

2. Vladimir Jankélévitch: *La mort* (Paris: Flammarion, 1967). Jean Baechler: *Les Suicides* (Paris: Calmann-Levy, 1975). Baechler's book has since been translated into German and is also available in a somewhat abridged version in English as *Suicides*, trans. Barry Cooper (New York: Basic Books, 1979).

I. BEFORE THE LEAP

1. Améry quotes from the German translation of Alvarez's book, Part III, which is called "The Closed World of Suicide."

2. In German Améry refers here to *Freitod* (suicide or, literally, free death; also voluntary death, as in the Roman *mors voluntarius*), *Suizid* (suicide), *Suizidant* (a suicide), and *Suizidär* (a suicidal person or a potential suicide). Of all these words only *Freitod* is an ordinary German word, but it is not used nearly as often as *Selbstmord* (self-murder). *Suizidant* and *Suizidär* could be rendered in English as "suicidant" and "suicidary," but that would be too stilted.

3. Pierre Drieu la Rochelle (1893–1945): French writer who collaborated with the Nazis during World War II.

4. Otto Weininger (1880–1903): Viennese author of *Geschlecht und Charakter* (*Sex and Character*), an anti-Semitic and misogynistic treatise that made a great impact on the German-speaking world when it was published in 1903. Weininger himself was Jewish.

5. P.F. refers to Paul Federn (1871–1950).

6. Cesare Pavese (1908–1950): Italian novelist and poet, who, two months after receiving the coveted Strega Prize, committed suicide over

his hapless love affair with a minor American movie actress, Constance Dowling. Paul Celan (1920–1970): poet, born in Czernowitz (at that time in Rumania), who wrote in German and lived in Paris; Peter Szondi (1929–1971): German literary scholar.

7. Lt. Gustl, main character of *Leutnant Gustl*, a novella by Arthur Schnitzler (1862–1931). The Prater is a large park in Vienna.

8. "Mattress sepulcher" (*Matratzengruft*): Heinrich Heine's name for his sickbed during the last years of his life in Paris. Heine did not commit suicide.

9. Heinrich von Kleist (1777–1811) killed himself in a suicide pact with Henriette Vogel, who wanted to die because of a painful and incurable disease; Thomas Chatterton (1752–1770) ended his life with poison.

10. From *Die Braut von Messina* (*The Bride of Messina*), Act IV, scene 10, by Friedrich Schiller (1759–1805).

11. Empedocles (ca. 485–425 B.C.E.): Greek philosopher who was supposed to have jumped into Mount Etna; Demosthenes (384–322 B.C.E.): Greek orator who took poison to avoid execution by political enemies; Cato, known as Cato the Republican (95–46 B.C.E.), committed suicide rather than submit to Julius Caesar; Buddhist monks who set themselves on fire: this occurred during the war in Vietnam as protest against the South Vietnamese government; Stefan Zweig (1881–1942): Viennese writer who committed suicide in Brazil in exile from Nazi Germany; Henri Montherlant (1868–1971): French novelist.

12. Allusion to *The Confessions of Felix Krull, Confidence Man* by Thomas Mann (1875–1955).

13. These two statements and the one that follows are from Ludwig Wittgenstein: *Tractatus logico-philosophicus* (Frankfurt am Main: Suhrkamp, 1960), propositions 6.5 and 7, translated here by J. D. B.

14. Walter Hasenclever (1890–1940): German writer who killed himself in France to escape the Nazis. Ernest Hemingway (1899–1961) killed himself with a shotgun.

15. Golo Mann (1909–1994), a historian, and Klaus Mann (1906–1949), a writer, were both sons of Thomas Mann. Klaus committed suicide.

16. Allusion to proposition 5.6 of Wittgenstein's *Tractatus*.

II. HOW NATURAL IS DEATH?

1. "Über einem Grabe" (Over a grave) by Conrad Ferdinand Meyer (1825–1898).

2. Gérard Philipe lived from 1922 to 1959, Georg Büchner from

1813 to 1837. Joachim Ziemssen is a character in *The Magic Mountain* by Thomas Mann.

3. Ernst Bloch, author of *The Principle of Hope*, lived more than ninety years (1885–1977); T. W. Adorno (1903–1969) died suddenly of a heart attack.

4. Ernst Haeckel (1834–1919): German zoologist.

5. The *Abitur* is an examination taken at the end of one's pre-college schooling in German-speaking countries to qualify for admission to a university; the *Abiturient* is a candidate for the examination or one who has just passed it.

6. Possibly a reference to a viciously negative review of Améry's *Lefeu* that was the cause of a persistent and long-lasting depression (See Marcel Reich-Ranicki, "Schrecklich ist die Verführung zum Roman," in *Franfurter Allgemeine Zeitung*, 1 January 1974).

7. I have used Barry Cooper's translation of Jean Baechler's *Suicides* for the passages quoted here, but other pasages from Baechler's book have been translated directly from Améry's German text.

8. Another character in *The Magic Mountain*.

9. Probably a reference to Martin Heidegger (1889–1976).

10. Allusion to *Henry IV* by Luigi Pirandello (1867–1936).

11. Allusion to a German folksong, "Es ist ein Schnitter, heißt der Tod" ("There is a reaper, his name is Death").

III. TO LAY HANDS ON ONESELF

1. Ingeborg Bachmann (1926–1973), Austrian poet and novelist important to Améry, was working on a cycle of novels and stories called *Ways of Death* when she died. Only one novel from the cycle, *Malina*, and a collection of five stories, *Three Paths to the Lake*, were completed, both of which have been translated into English. The remaining fragments have been published in German.

2. Yukio Mishima (1925–1970) committed ritual suicide, as he had promised, on the day he completed his tetralogy, *The Sea of Fertility*.

3. Allusion to the poem "Herbst" ("Autumn") by Rainer Maria Rilke (1875–1926).

4. Allusion to the poem "Hyperions Schicksalslied" ("Hyperion's Song of Destiny") by Friedrich Hölderlin (1770–1843).

5. Edmund Husserl (1859–1958): German philosopher; Maurice Merleau-Ponty (1908–1961): French philosopher.

6. Allusion to *Faust*, Part I, line 784, by Johann Wolfgang Goethe (1749–1832).

7. Allusion to *Der Mann im Monde* (The Man in the Moon), a novel by Wilhelm Hauff (1802–1827).

8. Allusion to the poem "Patmos" by Hölderlin.

IV. BELONGING TO ONESELF

1. Paul Ludwig Landsberg (1901–1944) was a student of the phenomenologist Max Scheler (1874–1928). Arnold Metzger (1892–1974) wrote on existentialism, particularly regarding freedom and death. Landsberg's reflections on death and suicide were written in French (*Essai sur l'expérience de la mort*, Paris, 1940).

2. Elias Canetti (1905–1994) wrote about survival in *Crowds and Power* and in the essay "Power and Survival," included in *The Conscience of Words*.

3. Allusion to Goethe's poem "An den Mond" ("To the Moon").

4. The poem by Hermann Hesse (1877–1962) is called "Bruder Tod" ("Brother Death").

5. Ingeborg Bachmann was severely burned in a fire in her apartment in Rome and died three weeks later. There were rumors about a suicide attempt. It is probable that the prescription drugs she had been taking contributed to her death.

6. Allusion to the line in Sartre's play *No Exit*, "Hell is—other people."

7. Allusion to the poem "Schlummerlied" ("Lullaby") by Richard Beer-Hoffmann (1866–1945).

V. THE ROAD TO THE OPEN

1. Améry does not quote the statement accurately here; he quotes it correctly in the first chapter (see note 13 to Chapter I).

2. From Heine's poem, "Morphine."

3. The last three sentences are given by Améry in English.

4. Allusion to the poem "Pidder Lüng" by Detlev von Liliencron (1844–1909).

5. Allusion to Schiller's *Don Carlos*, Act III, scene 8.

6. The negative view of Schnitzler that troubles Améry here has abated since Améry wrote this passage. Incidentally, the title of Schnitzler's novel and this chapter is *Der Weg ins Freie* in German. Améry plays on the meanings of the word *frei* and its compounds throughout this book and especially in this chapter in ways that cannot be translated without losing the wordplay. *Frei* can mean basically the same as the English word *free*, but it can also mean *voluntary*, as in *Freitod*. *Freiheit* can mean *freedom* and *liberty*, *Befreiung* means *liberation*, and when we

talk about being "out in the open" or going to it, the German word for *the open* is *das Freie*.

7. Allusion to the poem "Man frage nicht, was all die Zeit ich machte" ("Let no one ask what I was doing all the time") by Karl Kraus (1874–1936).

8 . Theodor Lessing (1872–1933): German writer about philosophy.

9. Theodor Körner (1791–1813), a prolific writer, once famous not only for his writing but for his patriotic death in the Napoleonic wars; Theodor Kramer (1897–1958) and Ernst Waldinger (1896–1970) were poets.

10. Golo Mann wrote a long historical study of Albrecht Wallenstein (1583–1634), general in the Thirty Years War and subject of Schiller's trilogy *Wallenstein*, at the end of which he says, just before his death, "I think I'll take a long sleep" (*Wallenstein's Death*, Act IV, scene 5).

11. Norbert von Hellingrath (1888–1916) was one of the first serious editors of Hölderlin's works and Pierre Bertaux (1907–) is a French scholar of German literature who has written extensively about Hölderlin.

12. From the poem "An die Nachgeborenen," known in English as "To Posterity," by Bertolt Brecht (1898–1956), based on a poem by the fifteenth-century French poet François Villon.

13. A play on words based on Hegel's assertion that the true is the whole.

Jean Améry (1921–1978) was born in Vienna and in 1938 emigrated to Belgium, where he joined the Resistance Movement. He was captured by the Nazis in 1943, tortured by the SS, and survived the next two years in the concentration camps. He was author of sixteen volumes of essays and an essayistic novel. He committed suicide in 1978.

John D. Barlow is Dean Emeritus of the School of Liberal Arts and Professor Emeritus of English and German at Indiana University–Purdue University at Indianapolis. He is author of *German Expressionist Film* and several translations, including Jean Améry's *On Aging*.